DRAW NIGH UNTO GOD

Draw Nigh Unto God

An Intimate Relationship with the Father

By Marilyn Haydel

Marilyn Haydel is the founder of *Ashes to Beauty Ministries* and, *The REAL (Respect~Encourage~Admonish~Love)* which is a forum for everyone dealing with real-life issues to know the truth of God's word from his perspective. She is currently a disciple of Unfailing Love Worship Center, where she serves beside her husband, Apostle Donald J. Haydel, Jr. They have four beautiful children. For more information Ms. Haydel can be reach at unfailing_love@outlook.com.

Copyright © 2020 Marilyn Haydel. All rights reserved.
Published by PurposeHouse Publishing, Columbia, Maryland.
Cover design by PurposeHouse Publishing, all rights reserved.
Printed in the USA

No part of this publication may be reproduced or distributed in any form or by any means, or stored in a database or retrieval system, without the prior written permission of the publisher. Requests for permission should be emailed to ministeringpurpose@gmail.com.

ISBN: 978-1-7329549-1-5

Unless otherwise indicated, all scriptural quotations are from the King James Version of the Bible.

Scripture from the Aramaic Bible in Plain English, Copyright © 2013 by SCL. All rights reserved.

Scripture from New American Standard Bible, Copyright © 1995 by the Lockman Foundation, All rights reserved.

Scripture from New King James Version, Copyright © 1982 by Thomas Nelson, Inc. All rights reserved.

Scripture from the New International Version, Copyright © 1973, 1978, 1984 by Biblica.

Scripture from the New Living Translation, Copyright © 1996, 2004 by Tyndale Charitable Trust.

Contents

Acknowlegements ix

Introduction 3

Chapter 1: If My People 5

Chapter 2: Self-Awareness Through Self-Examination ... 15

Chapter 3: A Heart of Repentance 23

Chapter 4: Power of Forgiveness 33

Chapter 5: Deliverance is the Children's Bread 39

Chapter 6: Religion versus Relationship 49

Chapter 7: Strengthening our Relationship with the Father 61

Chapter 8: God's Purpose for a Relationship 69

Chapter 9: Remaining Steadfast in God 81

Conclusion 97

My Prayer for You 101

About the Author 105

Acknowledgements

First and foremost, all glory and honor belong to God. I am so grateful to the Father, the Son, and the Holy Ghost for being my way maker and for the power of His amazing grace and love.

I want to thank every spiritual leader: apostles, pastors, bishops, the five-fold ministry gifts, and the ministry of helps. Thanks to each of you for the teaching, training, and equipping. You have helped me to continue in love and faith, and to remain steadfast to do the work of the ministry.

To every believer, non-believer, and coworker that I have met along the way, thank you for your part in shaping my life.

To my friends, thanks for understanding and accepting me for who I am. And thank you for respecting the call of God on my life. Thank you for being *real* in my life.

To my mother, one of the strongest, wonderful, and most loveable and encouraging women in the world, you are a virtuous and blessed woman of God. You have given so much of yourself not only to your children but to all of God's children. You are the epitome of loving like Jesus in the lives of many. You wear the crown of wisdom and compassion. Thanks, mom!

To my siblings, and their spouses and children, and my extended sisters, what a blessing to be part of a family that enjoys one another. The outpouring of love is limitless. I cherish every moment that we are together, which are filled with so much joy and laughter. We are a blessed family, and I thank each of you for all that you have contributed to my life.

To every uncle, aunt, niece, nephew, and cousin and extended family member, thank you for being a part of my life.

To my children, you are truly a gift from God, and I thank God each day for trusting me to train and admonish you in his ways. I thank God for your differences; each of you has helped me to become better. Thank you for allowing me to be a mom and share myself with you.

To the most amazing and mighty man of valor, my husband, my love, my confidant, and friend, I thank you for allowing me to be me. Thank you for *always* supporting and standing with me since the first day we met. And here we are twenty-two years later, yet *Living Out Our Vows Everyday (LOVE)*. You make my work in the marriage as a wife and mother an easy task. Thanks for continuously covering and washing me in the word of God. I love you, and I am yet *in* love with you.

Finally, to all of you who will read this book, thank you for listening to the voice of God and drawing nigh unto Him. I declare God's greatness upon your life, and may your relationship with the Father become more intimate each day.

Thanks, and shalom to all!

Gratefully,

Marilyn Haydel

Draw Nigh Unto God: An Intimate Relationship with the Father

Introduction

For the past eleven years, God has been speaking to me about writing a book. Throughout this course of time, he had me watch and pray, and would whisper, "That is a chapter for the book." He gave me the title and the words for the book, but not a release. Little did I know, when I went into prayer on October 21, 2019, with a heavy heart and crying out to him, that he would say to me, "Write the book." It was a shocking surprise because it wasn't either of the books that he had spoken previously. But as he spoke, I listened. That night, the birthing of "Draw Nigh unto God" began. I was in awe as he began to speak, and the revelation began to pour out. The tears kept pouring as he continued speaking. He kept reiterating that unless his people draw nigh unto him, they would not be able to withstand the complexity of the times and the seasons of their lives. (the hour that is upon us now). "The enemy is at work, but my people must know that I am much greater, I am calling them to me!" he said.

During the next few months, he spoke each chapter. I didn't understand it all, but I kept writing. And as I continued, it all became clearer. I, too, was going through a period of asking, "What is happening, God?" I asked, "What is happening in the world, my walk, within the local church, and body of Christ?" The more God spoke, the gladness I had, because he was speaking, was overshadowed by grief because I realized that I was listening to a broken heart.

It is so important that we position ourselves to a lifestyle of consistently drawing nigh unto him. I explain why, as well as the purpose and benefits of drawing nigh to him in each chapter.

It is in his presence that God will reveal and give us strategies, instructions, guidance. He will reveal:

- The dos and the don'ts by which we are to live our lives
- How we are to combat the wiles of the enemy, to intercede for the world and others
- How to be a witness for him

His presence is a place of sustainment, comfort, protection, refuge, love, joy, peace, and strength. Everything we need is in his presence and accompanied by his word. As the first partaker of this book, my life is forever changed. Now, I live from the greater position that God has for each of us in Him. The spiritual warfare that comes by the ways of Satan's tactics, schemes, devices of persecution, accusations, trials, and tribulations have not ceased. But it has been conquered!

This book is not about steps or methods for drawing nigh unto God but rather to declare the message that was given to me by God. Only God can order the steps of your life. I pray that your heart will be open to what the Spirit of God is saying and accept the challenges at the end of each chapter as an act of obedience unto God.

I declare God's greatness for your life as he has already chosen, predestined, and ordained for you!

Shalom

Chapter 1: If My People

The outlook was grim. "The world is rapidly decaying," I cried. "My people must begin to draw nigh unto me," a still small voice responded.

As a prophet of God, there are times when my spirit grieves. During this prayer time, I was praying for the world. We are witnessing countless murders; division and disunity is tearing everyone apart in the world, the local church, and the body of Christ. There is bullying in our schools, suicide among our children, and marriages are being destroyed, etc. I wept that night in prayer for our country and leaders.

I remember thinking, "God, the world is decaying," Immediately, I heard the voice of God speak, "Marilyn, I am yet in control, but unless my people draw nigh unto me and seek my face, the world will continue to be in the state that it is in." The more I cried out to him, the more he revealed that the time has come where he is calling his people to draw nigh unto him.

Throughout the next three months and forevermore, God is seeking for a people that will draw nigh unto him. As we draw nigh unto him, he promises to draw nigh unto us and lead and guide us in every area of lives.

> Therefore say thou unto them, Thus saith the Lord of hosts; Turn ye unto me, saith the Lord of hosts, and I will turn unto you, saith the Lord of hosts. (Zechariah 1:3 KJV)

During this time, the Holy Spirit spoke about the importance of drawing nigh unto the Father and establishing a personal, intimate relationship with him. A relationship that is built on prayer, self-examination, repentance, forgiveness, and deliverance. What is important is a personal, intimate relationship not religion; a relationship that comes through the ministry of Jesus' redemption, reconciliation, and restoration. A relationship with the Father causes a renewing of the mind. Through a personal, intimate relationship with the Father, we experience his love, mercy, and grace. We draw nigh through praise and worship; and establish a solid foundation that will keep us steadfast in him.

Throughout the chapters of this book, I will share what the Spirit of the Lord spoke to me, along with how God has kept and is yet keeping me, as I continue to draw nigh unto him. A relationship is built as you commune with him, getting to know *him* not know *of* him.

For "If my people":

> *If my people, which are called by my name, shall humble themselves, and pray, and seek my face, and turn from their wicked ways; then will I hear from heaven, and will forgive their sin, and will heal their land. (2 Chronicles 7:14 KJV)*

Prayer is my testimony.

During prayer that night, the Holy Spirt brought 2 Chronicles 7:14 to my remembrance, "If my people, which are called by my name, shall humble themselves, and pray, and seek my face, and turn from their wicked ways; then will I hear from heaven, and will forgive their sin, and will heal their land." In this text, God gives us four responsibilities: humility, praying, seeking, and turning. I will speak on each of them, but first, look at a key element for a personal relationship, which is prayer.

Prayer is my testimony, and I recall as a little girl, my grandmother would always say that whatever we were going through, or whatever we need, just call on the name of the Lord. She would say that I could pray to God, and he will answer. That always stuck with me throughout my life. Prayer became my way of escape in many situations and circumstances, and I want to point out to whoever may be reading this book and feeling that they don't know God like that or know how to pray, that God hears the cry of his people. I was not saved, and I didn't know God, but God answered me; and if he did it for me, he will do it for you.

As I grew in God, prayer became less about me but more about God's desires, and others. As I pointed out in 2 Chronicles 7:14, we must have a burden to pray for the people of God, Jerusalem, the world, and our nation, President, government, and spiritual leaders. We must learn to give more of ourselves to let mankind, saved and unsaved, know how much God loves them and is concerned about them. The time has come, now more than ever, that we must get away from our opinionated judgment and condemnation, which keeps us in a state of more talking and less prayer.

That which was lost was revealed.

As I was praying John 3:16, when Jesus came to save that which was lost, I heard, "What is the "that" which was lost?" At that moment, revelation came. That which was lost was a relationship with the Father, the purpose for which Jesus came to reconcile us back to the Father. As believers, we focus on the lost, and we should. But the Holy Spirit whispered that a person can be saved, serving in the church, and yet not have a *relationship* with God. I thought of us as believers and where we are.

Salvation is a gift, and just because we believe and confess Jesus, that does not constitute a relationship. Think about your relationships and how they were formed. You had to spend time with the person, get to know them, talk to them, and listen to them. When the revelation came to me, it changed my life because I went through a period where I was doing church, busy with church duties, having a good time praising, yet I was feeling an emptiness and void.

I remember when God spoke to me and showed me how and where I got off course, which I will discuss more later. But I shared that to say; yes, it can happen to us as saved, sanctified, born-again believers. We can get off track.

As I continued in prayer, reading John 3:16, I heard the still small voice say, "What does John 3:17 say?" Immediately God begin to speak to my heart, "I did not send my son into the world to condemn the world, but that the world through him might be saved." I pondered on how much condemnation there was in the church. And if God did not send his son into the world to condemn the world, but that the world through him might be saved, where and how did we get off course?

I thought back to past conversations, and yes, some of my own conversations. I could see how easy it is to condemn people. As I drew nigh unto him, it was unfolded that condemnation is driven by the lack of love we have for one another, and it is driving people further and further away from him. All I could think of at that moment was the blood of Jesus, and that his blood was shed for *everyone*.

God kept echoing that he longs for his people to draw nigh unto him, for their sake and the world's. It is so easy to judge and condemn people, and not even pray for them. We must know that as believers, we are accountable to pray and stand in the gap to prevent things from happening. But so often, we join in with the devil to condemn the world. We bring our opinions, self-righteous judgement, and condemnation.

However, 2 Chronicles 7:14 is clear stating, "If my people…" When we pray, God gives us his attention, opens heaven, and sends healing to the land, and his people. We desire God for ourselves, situations, and church services. We cry out for his Glory, but we must draw nigh unto him for others and the chaos that is taking place in the world. We must give more thought to the motivation of our prayers. Where and what is our focus?

We desire the Glory of God, but let me share a little nugget of wisdom—we should know that every time God sent his glory in the Bible, his glory came with a responsibility to do his will. It came with a responsibility to bring about a change in the environment and/or atmosphere. His glory is not a bragging right for the body of Christ, but for what God wants to accomplish.

God longs to hear our prayers as we draw nigh unto him. The more we see what is taking place in the world and the lives of his people, the more our focus should shift. It should never be on what we think isn't right about the world or someone, instead we should be driven to pray and intercede in line with the word of God. We are not to pray our will or what we think. No, true intercession is believing and trusting God and calling those things that be not as though they were—not according to our view, but according to God's word and desires.

In this hour, for such a time like this, God is calling for his children to draw nigh unto him. It is his desire to bring healing to the land and healing to the lives of his people. We can no longer be numb to what is happening in the world all around us. We have a responsibility that is written in 2 Chronicles 7:14, "If my people, which are called by my name, shall humble themselves, and pray, and seek my face, and turn from their wicked ways; then will I hear from heaven, and will forgive their sin, and will heal their land."

What does it mean to draw nigh unto God?

Drawing nigh to God is coming to a place (a position) before him, seeking his face, thoughts, and plans. Realizing that only God knows the beginning and the end, it is important that we become more thirsty and hungry for God and what he desires. We must hunger and thirst for what God wants for our life and family, the local church, the body of Christ, the world, and everyone in it. We don't want one person to be missed or left behind. God is patiently waiting, and my message to all is, as it is written in Zechariah 1:3 NASB, "Therefore say to them, 'Thus says the Lord of hosts, "Return to Me," declares the Lord of hosts, "that I may return to you," says the Lord of hosts."

God desires for all to come, and more so, for believers to come not only as one person but also as a unified body with the same purpose and in the same Spirit. One person's obedience is powerful and can make a difference, but can you imagine what the manifestation of the power of God will be like on Earth when the whole body of Christ comes together as one? One Lord, one Faith and one Baptism. The innumerable benefits of the kingdom are available as we draw nigh unto God.

Know that God's arms are outstretched towards his people; he is speaking in this hour, and will be forevermore, that we must come closer to him in prayer. We must have an ear to hear and a heart to obey. Prayer is bigger than us and what we desire. We can't spend all our time trying to obtain things from God but never becoming more like Jesus. It is so easy to be swept away during our daily lives. We are faced with fiery times, trials, and the persecution of this world. We can find ourselves existing and living each day, but not living from that place of prayer, where we have been predestined and ordained by God for his great use.

We have a responsibility to draw near.

Our responsibility is to call heaven to earth, to let God's kingdom come on earth as it is in heaven, and to call those things that be not as though they were. We must use the authority given us to speak things into existence, declaring "Let there be!" Just as Adam was given authority to name things, we have authority to declare things. Jesus was given authority over us (John 17:2) and he gave us the keys of the kingdom to bind and loose (Matthew 16:19).

> As thou hast given him power over all flesh, that he should give eternal life to as many as thou hast given him. (John 17:2 KJV)

> And I will give unto thee the keys of the kingdom of heaven: and whatsoever thou shalt bind on earth shall be bound in heaven: and whatsoever thou shalt loose on earth shall be loosed in heaven. (Matthew 16:19 KJV)

What are we speaking when we see the will of God not being manifested on the earth, the people of God not in their proper position in Christ, and lost souls running away from the church versus running to the church? What are we speaking to our perceptions, ideas, and opinions? What are we doing with our keys? Are we locking or unlocking doors in our lives and the lives of others? Do we know how and what to bind and loose?

As we continue in our daily lives, we must pay close attention to how we are spending our days. We must ask ourselves what impact we are having on others, and are we using our influence in a positive way. We need to evaluate whether we are getting lost and/or getting off course by the things we see and don't see, hear and don't hear, and do or do not do. We must be honest with ourselves.

It is time for us to stop for a moment and take a spiritual inventory of where we are. This requires self-examination so that we can become more alert and aware of what we need to do. As we draw nigh unto God, a relationship with him quickens us to pray and intercede more for others, and the things that concerns God.

Drawing Nigh Chapter Challenge

Commit to a week to draw nigh unto God and to listen. Seek God's desires. During this time pray, for our leaders (spiritual and government), our government, the body of Christ, lost souls, backsliders, and those that are hurt and broken. Do not be moved by your opinions and thoughts, and do not allow what you think to rule your thoughts. Decide to love and show love to all mankind. Ask God for a broken and contrite spirit and to be a vessel for him in all you do. Reflect on what Jesus did for you on the cross. Walk in humility and lowliness of heart.

Chapter 2: Self-Awareness Through Self-Examination

We identify where we are through self-examination and self-awareness. As I look back over my life, I can't begin to tell you how often I have had to take a spiritual inventory. It especially happens when I find myself thinking on things that are not true, honest, just, pure, lovely, and of good report (Philippians 4:8). You know, those things for which we so often want to blame others.

In life, it is important that we are aware of our spiritual state of being. When we are not aware of our self, it is easy to go through life not reaching our fullest potential. We can easily get off-course and conform to the world and the world systems. And we can be completely ignorant or oblivious to God's desires for our lives. We can lose ourselves, and where we are mentally and spiritually in our walk with God or in our everyday life. Have you ever asked yourself why you feel the way you do, or why you do what you do?

When I find myself feeling like Paul when he wrote in Romans 7:19-21 KJV, "For the good that I would I do not: but the evil which I would not, that I do. Now if I do that I would not, it is no more I that do it, but sin that dwelleth in me. I find then a law, that, when I would do good, evil is present with me." When this happens in my life, I know I must draw nigh unto God for a cleansing. Whether you are a believer of God or not, evil is present all around; if you are not aware of your actions and what causes them, you can find yourself making detrimental decisions and choices that are outside of the character of God and what he desires for you.

Why is inventory so important?

In a physical store, inventory is related to the important task of maintaining the right quantity of goods, and timing for replenishment based on a deep understanding of customer demands for the product. Likewise, in the Spirit, it is important for us to maintain a right-standing with our Father, so we can have a deeper understanding of his demands for our lives. Everyone is born with a purpose and a plan that has already been predestined and ordained by God. It is when we take spiritual inventory of our lives that we can determine whether we are fulfilling that purpose, and reaching our fullest potential in Christ. We can also determine what we are doing or not doing that has become hindrances in our lives. At times, we must look at the contributing factors to our behavior and actions.

As I speak with people, and in particular ladies, of all ages and race, I have come to find that we know how to justify our actions—what we do and why we do it. Some of our reasons may be valid, but for most of my conversations with others or with myself, the justification is more often an excuse. We must be honest with ourselves, which is the key element as we draw nigh unto God.

As we draw nigh unto him, God will reveal us to ourselves and show us areas in our lives where we are not lining up to all he has for us. God's greatest demand is for our character to become like his. It is so easy to get caught up in our agendas, desires and the work of the ministry. But those things do not profit us if our character does not line up with God's. We must operate from a place of integrity and honesty as it relates to the word of God. God's love for us is authentic, genuine and unconditional; there are no conditions to earn God's love. Jesus already did that, which I will discuss later.

But there are conditions, ifs and buts throughout the word of God for living in righteousness. He tells us what and how we are to live, what and how we are to do, and most of all, how we are to live with and respond to one another. Notice I said respond, not react—there is a difference.

Self-examination and self-awareness are key.

Self-awareness is a time of being honest and true with oneself as we draw nigh unto God. Our opinions of ourselves can be distorted because we do not like to confess that our opinions do not always come from a place of justice and pureness. I would like to encourage each of you as you read this book, to stop, take the time, and conduct an inventory of your life. It is something that should be done more often than one may think. If more than three months have gone since you last took the time to really take a good look at where you are, it is time. I know for myself; I know it is time when I find my thoughts are all over the place and emotions are either at an all-time high or low. When I allow my thought patterns to wander outside of God's character, I have to do a "checkmate". Checkmate is the term God gave to me for myself, and sometimes I can hear his still small voice whisper "Checkmate, Marilyn."

Why is it important to do a self-examination? Because in this world we are face with so many things, day-to-day conversations, jobs, families, spouses, children, friends, co-workers, places, and things in general. If done honestly, self-inventory is a sure way to keep you on the straight and narrow and to keep you from straying to the left or right.

Spiritual inventory, if honestly done, teaches us about you. It can help you understand you and it allows you to see and identify your weakness, strengths, and behaviors. Areas in our lives that needs improvement. We can then, evaluate where we are according to God's word and where we need to be and how and what we need to do. Conducting inventory is only about yourself. It is not about others or others' actions or what has been done or not done to you. It is completely the only time that you can be selfish to look at you and take responsibility for where you are and the things that God will reveal. It is not a time for pointing the finger or saying if "this or that" would have happened "then I wouldn't have done this or that." No, it is all about you accepting responsibility for whatever God is revealing and you wanting to make every effort to surrender and yield to God for him to change you. Uh oh, did I say the bad words "surrendering and yielding." Yes, as you draw nigh unto God, it will require you surrendering and yielding to God. It is a good position in God, and it also a form of humility.

Honesty and humility are very important when doing self-examination. We must be truthful about our thoughts, will, and emotions. Honesty requires openness in your communication with God, and humility requires admitting that you are messed up. At the age of 32, I went through one of the worst times of my life, where I just cried up and out; yes, up and out. That was the first time that I heard the audible voice of God, and I can still hear the words he spoke on that day. I had been in and out of church since I was twelve, but I never knew that God speaks or would speak to someone who was messed up in sin. I want to encourage that one person who may be thinking that God is not listening or doesn't care. He does! From that day, I had a choice to make. I was no longer going to "do church," but I would become the church. Now at the age of fifty-eight, I do not hesitate to run and draw nigh unto him. Someone once asked me who I talk to when I need someone. I had to stop because I had never thought about it. Drawing nigh to God—not another person—and allowing him to wash and cleanse me from my thoughts, will, and emotions had become the norm, and God gets all the glory. Yes, I still have issues and make mistakes, but I have learned where and who to run to for the truth about me.

Self-examination requires that you want to know the truth about yourself and your life. Our heavenly Father is the only one that knows us, it is he who created us and knows the plan and purpose for our lives. He knows why we think like we think and do what we do. There is nothing more pleasing to God, than when we position ourselves in his presence, naked before him. It is a place of safety, where you can let your guard down, take off any mask and be yourself; a place where you are not judged or condemned but where he can speak into your every need. Yes, sometimes it comes with correction and rebuke. I am a witness that God's love is still true and sweet even during his correction—unlike man or the lack of love to which we grow accustomed. He knows how to correct and yet make you feel good about who you are because you know that you are created in his image. As you open up, God will reveal you to you, him to you, and areas of your life where growth is needed. He reveals things we must let go and sometimes people we must let go. Letting go of people can be hard, but God will give you a way to escape and how to let go. Having to let go of people is not always because they did anything to you. It sometimes can be that God will reveal that some people are in our lives for only a season and for a reason so we can become. We are the ones that get ourselves attached to people. I am so grateful to all of the people that God has allowed to cross my path. Many have come through my military career and the body of Christ. In my natural mind, there was some that I would be okay if I don't ever see again, but God had to reveal the hidden things in my heart that now I can testify of the appreciation that I have towards people. Once again, drawing nigh to him and doing that "checkmate," that letting go became easy. And for some, perhaps a later chapter of my life will cause us to unite again, but it will be in God's timing and will.

In this thing called life, we are faced with so much that if we do not do a self-examination, we can easily get loss in all the day-to-day activities and ins and outs of this world. However, we know that we are to be in this world but not of this world, that does not keep the world from attaching itself or sometimes attacking. Hebrews 10:22 KJV says, "let us draw near to God with a sincere heart and with the full assurance that faith brings, having our hearts sprinkled to cleanse us from a guilty conscience and having our bodies washed with pure water."

Self-awareness through self-examination requires you to be real with yourself. Open up to God. He is gentle, generous, and genuine. His love is so sweet, and as you draw nigh unto him, you will experience his love, joy and peace and in turn you will desire to walk in his love, joy, and peace towards others. God desires to refresh your soul and spirit. The more you open up in truth, the more you will become aware of who you are and who he is. You will know how you are to respond to God and to others versus reacting.

Self-awareness begins in the heart.

Our heart it is the one place that concerns God the most. In Psalm 51:17, his word lets us know that he loves a broken and contrite spirit; this is our sacrifice to him.

> The sacrifices of God are a broken spirit: a broken and a contrite heart, O God, thou wilt not despise. (Psalm 51:14 KJV)

A few years ago, when I was in prayer, the Holy Spirit spoke to me about spiritual self-inventory, what I now refer to as "checkmate." It is a period where I have to stop and take a look at myself, my thoughts, and my actions. If I am in a place of reacting versus responding to things that go on around me, I know it is time to allow God to check my heart. In my life, when it seems like nothing is going right, I recognize that I have allowed too much time to lapse without taking inventory. Inventory brings us to a state of awareness. According to Merriam Webster's dictionary, inventory is a product or item which can be specified as stock or an asset that is purchased for sale or resale. So spiritually, we can see that we are God's inventory. We too have been purchased by the blood of Jesus and set apart for God's great use. We are God's property, and our lives must be inventoried, examined to make ourselves readily available for his use.

As I stated at the beginning of this chapter, self-awareness begins in the heart, the one place that concerns God the most (our heart). It requires humility and a broken and contrite spirit.

In Psalm 51:17, his word lets us know that he loves a broken and contrite spirit; this is our sacrifice to him. He will not reject a broken and a repentant heart. A repentant heart brings refreshing in our lives, but the fullness comes with an act of change. We have heard that change is inevitable, that is true in the natural and the spirit. We must be willing to change so that we can become. Become more like Christ and become the person who God has created, predestined, and ordained while we were yet in our mother's womb.

Change begins with a heart of repentance. As we draw nigh unto God and open up, God will reveal the good, the bad, and the ugly. When this happens, it will require repentance and renouncing some things in our lives. I refer to the word "naked" a lot because nakedness is a vulnerable place, and we need to be more vulnerable in and with God versus allowing the enemy to use our vulnerabilities. As we draw nigh unto God, our relationship with him will grow to a place of truth, honesty, and humility.

Drawing Nigh Chapter Challenge

Take a day and be honest with yourself. Conduct a spiritual self-examination and be honest with God. Send a meeting request to yourself for the next couple of months. In prayer, ask God to search your heart for the hidden and wicked areas. Write them down.

Chapter 3: A Heart of Repentance

Drawing nigh unto God requires a heart of repentance. Let us not fool ourselves; God's word is the truth, and it says that "For all have sinned, and come short of the glory of God." (Romans 3:23 KJV) and "If we say that we have no sin, we deceive ourselves, and the truth is not in us." (1 John 1:8 KJV) Because we are still being perfected and maturing in the things of God, we fall short, make mistakes, and have issues with which we are dealing. And all of that does not always produce our best behavior, or more importantly, God's character. The word of God tells us in Acts: 3: 19 KJV, "Repent ye therefore, and be converted, that your sins may be blotted out, when the times of refreshing shall come from the presence of the Lord." There is a refreshing that takes place when we repent. Although we are not supposed to be conformed to the world, we do find ourselves giving in to the things and behaviors of the world.

A heart of repentance draws us closer in our relationship with the Father. Confessing our sins, seeking God's help, and allowing the Holy Spirit to change us from the inside out is priceless. It is a sweet aroma in which God takes pleasure.

Repentance is not condemnation.

The word repent has become so distorted by religion and used as a weapon for all the wrong reasons of controlling and manipulation that it makes a person feel so dirty, guilty, and hopeless. Repentance is acknowledging your wrongdoing, being remorseful, having sincere and genuine regret for the wrong that you have done, having a desire to stop and to turn away from the sin.

People can be argumentative when the subject of repentance comes up. I have heard over and over that you have not repented until you have stopped the act or behavior. Throughout my walk, I have watched people hurting and doing their best only to be told, you haven't repented because you keep doing the same thing over and over. People say things like, you don't mean it. If you did, you would stop. I have seen the spirit of condemnation make people feel ashamed. My heart would break.

One day during a church service, the Holy Spirit whispered, "Marilyn repentance is also a process." A person cannot always stop their actions by themselves, that the purpose for which I was sent. I am *the Helper*. It made sense. If we could stop all our sinful ways by ourselves, there would not have been a need for Jesus or for him to send the Holy Spirit. If we could automatically stop every wrong behavior in our lives, we would not have needed Jesus nor the blood of Jesus that was shed for the remission of our sins.

Yes, at some point, stopping must happen. But often, when I talk to people about repenting, they feel helpless because their behavior didn't stop right away. God gives us his grace, **not** to sin or to continue in sin, but to give us an avenue for his change to take place in our heart. Don't run away from God; run to him. I had to learn to do that when I could feel the spirit of condemnation working against me. I had to submit to God and resist the enemy—even if the enemy was me. But I had to lean on the Holy Spirit. I realized that I couldn't do it on my own.

Repentance is a renewing of the mind to God's perspective.

We must recognize and regret our behavior, and seek God's forgiveness. As we draw nigh, we must be truthful about the sin in our lives. We draw nigh with clean hands and a pure heart. Psalm 24: 3-5 KJV says, "Who shall ascend into the hill of the Lord? or who shall stand in his holy place? He that hath clean hands, and a pure heart; who hath not lifted up his soul unto vanity, nor sworn deceitfully. He shall receive the blessing from the Lord, and righteousness from the God of his salvation."

Because we are yet being perfected (maturing in the things of God), we will fall short at times. The key is to immediately repent and ask God to change you so that you can become more like Christ. Although we are not supposed to conform to the world, we do find ourselves giving in to the things and behaviors of the world. This is not a reason to continue in your sin—I repeat this is not a reason to continue in your sin!

What I want you to know is that you have a helper, and his name is the Holy Spirit. If you desire to change in your heart, the Holy Spirit will help you as you draw nigh unto him. A heart of brokenness will lead us to a prayer of righteousness that motivates us to a place repentance.

A heart of brokenness will lead us to a prayer of righteousness that motivates us to a place repentance.

Honesty is also a part of repentance. It takes honesty to acknowledge your need for repentance, because repentance involves announcing and renouncing those areas of bad behavior in your life. When I had my first child out of wedlock, I had to confess, denounce, and announce my sin. Confessing was me acknowledging the wrong I did, denouncing was me calling out the truth behind the sin, the spirit of sexual immorality, and that it was against God and his will for my life. Renouncing was me making up my mind that I was accepting responsibility for my actions, and I was not staying in it or that place of sin.

I also heard more teaching and studies on true repentance. Proverbs 28:13 NIV says, "Whoever conceals their sins does not prosper, but the one who confesses and renounces them finds mercy." I wanted to prosper, and I realized that I needed God's mercy. I am grateful, knowing that his mercy is new for me every morning. The more I begin to confess, denounce, and renounce my wrong doings and behavior, the more I realized that I was being freed, healed, delivered, and restored. As we yield and surrender, repentance allows God to make us whole and complete in him.

Believe on the word of God and the power of the blood of Jesus that washes and cleanses us. John 1:29b ESV says, "…Behold the Lamb of God who takes away the sins of the world!" We must know that this is what Jesus has done for us. We don't have to beat ourselves up when we make mistakes or need to change. Draw nigh unto God, repent, and ask the Holy Spirit to be your helper. The Holy Spirit will help you, and you must talk to the Holy Spirit as well. It is sad that the teaching of the Holy Spirit is lacking today. When I was taught and learned more about the Holy Spirit, and the reason for his coming and dwelling with us today, I knew I had a helper who I called my *best friend forever*.

When I was taught and learned more about the Holy Spirit, and the reason for his coming and dwelling with us today, I knew I had a helper who I called my best friend forever.

A heart of repentance draws us closer in our relationship with the Father. When we seek the Holy Spirit's help and allow him to change us, it is precious in the sight of God. It is a sweet aroma in which God takes pleasures.

It is so easily to be tricked and deceived by the enemy, and we can also deceive ourselves, thinking that there is no need to repent because we categorize our sin. Well, in God's eyes, sin is sin, and you may not be a murderer or a thief, but what about the lies, gossip, backbiting, or the corrupt and filthy communication that comes out of our mouths. No, not intentionally, but whether intentionally or not, it does not change the fact that repentance is needed in our lives.

God's word tells us that we all have sinned and fall short of his glory, (Romans 3:3) and if any man said that he has no sin, we deceive ourselves and the truth is no in us (1 John 1:8). But then, his word also says, "Let us therefore come boldly unto the throne of grace, that we may obtain mercy, and find grace to help in time of need." (Hebrews 4:16 KJV) The word lets us know that as we repent, God is the one who will bring a change and help us stop the behavior. Don't allow the enemy to keep you from repenting because you are having a hard time stopping, whatever your issue or behavior(s). God knows the motives of your heart. Draw nigh unto God and allow him to do and complete the work in you.

Our Father receives us just as we are. Even when we mess up, his love is unfailing towards us. We can take off the mask and be totally free in him. There is such a peace as we allow God to be our confidant. James 4:8 KJV says, "Draw nigh to God, and he will draw nigh to you. Cleanse your hands, ye sinners; and purify your hearts, ye double minded." Allow God to cleanse your hands and purify your hearts. The enemy would love to keep you in double-mindedness, going back and forth, telling you that there is no need to repent. God will bring clarity to your lives when you draw nigh unto him. Throughout my life, I have found that place of security in him. The word of God tells us that we are not to be ignorant of Satan's devices, tricks, and tactics. And one of Satan's tactics is to make you believe that you can't come to the Father or repent because an issue is still in your life. Let your heart and motives be pure before God and watch God!

Trust God. Whether you feel like you need or don't need him in a situation, he desires to hear you in all things. I encourage you and challenge you to always go before God. He cares so much about what and how you are feeling. Draw nigh unto him and listen as he gently whispers an answer and gives you a strategy to overcome or stop the behavior altogether.

I will never forget a strategy that the Holy Spirit gave me. You have heard that God hath chosen the foolish things of the world to confound the wise, and God hath chosen the weak things of the world to confound the things which are mighty (1 Corinthians 1:2). The Holy Spirit said to me, "Thank Satan for reminding you just how good God is." And for me, it has been a sure way of defeating him every time. I reflected on the blood of Jesus and the price that only he has paid for me. At first, people looked at me strangely when I used this strategy, but they weren't in my room with me when God was moving. Even to this day, when the enemy raises his ugly head and tries to make me feel unworthy, I stand tall and say, "Thank you devil for reminding me how Good my God is." Meaning, God loves us even when we don't feel or think he does. Then I run into God's outstretched arms that he has extended to me and receive help in the time of all my needs. I encourage you when you think or feel that you can't draw nigh, know that God's word is true. He is not going to leave you or forsake you (Hebrews 13:5). Give God a chance! Repent and continue to have a heart of repentance.

As a result of drawing nigh to God, I realized that through my many ups and downs, mess ups and failures, good, bad or indifferences, it was in his presence that I found my resting place. We can pour our heart out with our shortcomings, behaviors, and concerns, knowing that we will not be judged. Even at times when we need to be corrected and rebuked, the blessings and beauty of God's correction or rebuke is knowing that he has our best interest at heart. His correction comes from his character to get our character to line up with his.

Jesus has given us the rights and permission to come nigh to him. Hebrews 4:16 KJV says, "Let us therefore come boldly unto the throne of grace, that we may obtain mercy, and find grace to help in time of need." Like David, let us make Psalm 51 part of our lifestyle, where we repent and seek God for forgiveness.

> Have mercy upon me, O God, according to thy lovingkindness: according unto the multitude of thy tender mercies blot out my transgressions. Wash me thoroughly from mine iniquity and cleanse me from my sin. For I acknowledge my transgressions: and my sin is ever before me. Against thee, thee only, have I sinned, and done this evil in thy sight: that thou mightiest be justified when thou speakest, and be clear when thou judgest. Behold, I was shapen in iniquity; and in sin did my mother conceive me. Behold, thou desirest truth in the inward parts: and in the hidden part thou shalt make me to know wisdom. Purge me with hyssop, and I shall be clean: wash me, and I shall be whiter than snow. Make me to hear joy and gladness; that

the bones which thou hast broken may rejoice. Hide thy face from my sins and blot out all mine iniquities. Create in me a clean heart, O God; and renew a right spirit within me. Cast me not away from thy presence; and take not thy holy spirit from me. Restore unto me the joy of thy salvation; and uphold me with thy free spirit. Then will I teach transgressors thy ways; and sinners shall be converted unto thee. (Psalm 51 KJV)

I want to encourage you that nothing we do surprises our Father; he can handle our "its" in this thing called "Life." Our "its' are our issues, and it is our "its" that hinder us from becoming all that God desires for us to become. They hinder us from reaching our fullest potential in him. He is waiting to hear you share your "it" so he can in turn tell you how to get over "it." Let your prayer of repentance lead you to possess a lifestyle where your behaviors are directed by the leading of the Holy Spirit.

It is so easy to be tricked and deceived by the enemy. And we can deceive ourselves by thinking that there is no need to repent because we have categorized our sin. Well, in God's eyes sin is sin. You may not be a murderer or a thief, like the two men who were crucified with Jesus. But what about lying, gossiping, or the corrupt and filthy communication that comes out of our mouths? No, not intentionally, but whether intentionally or not, it does not change the fact that repentance is necessary. Your Father's arms are always outstretched towards you—even now. As we draw nigh unto him with a genuine heart of repentance, our relationship becomes pure.

Drawing Nigh Chapter Challenge

Take the list from Chapter 2, and repent. Be regretful and remorseful-- take a note of Psalm 51:4 which says, "Against you, and you alone, have I sinned; I have done what is evil in your sight." Ask the Holy Spirit to be your helper and to aide and guide you in your thoughts, actions, and responses. Be open and willing for God to deliver you.

Chapter 4: Power of Forgiveness

The power of forgiveness is a doorway to your freedom. Through forgiveness, God frees you and you also free yourself. There are over seventy scriptures in the Bible that talk about forgiveness. That lets you know forgiveness is important. The awesomeness of drawing nigh unto God is that he knows your heart and the hidden things in your heart.

When I rededicated my life to God, forgiveness was the first area that God dealt with me about. He showed me that I had not given any attention to the unforgiveness that was in my heart. Because it was from many years ago and I was a new creature in Christ, I just assumed I was good to go. I was going through life, I didn't understand how one thing had a domino effect on another area of my life. As I continued to draw nigh unto him, I was becoming more aware that not forgiving others was more detrimental to me than the people I was not forgiving. I didn't realize it at the time, but some of the symptoms such as bitterness, anger, resentment, bad attitudes, etc., were coming from the root of unforgiveness that I was harboring in my heart. Even though I was not giving it a thought, God knew it was buried and rooted, and it was something that I needed to release.

Do we have a right not to forgive? No! At times, when things were done to me, I thought I was legit by holding on, but God revealed that I had to let go. I can promise you, as you become honest and open to God through self-examination, God will reveal any unforgiveness in your life. Intentionally or not intentionally, we carry unforgiveness because we think that we have a right. The reality of life is that things happen to us, but we must never allow reality to take the place of the truth of God's word. People will hurt and disappoint you. But we must forgive. Choosing not to forgive not only causes separation from the person but also causes separation from God. It wasn't until God reminded me of the blood of Jesus and spoke to me that what I wanted from him I wasn't wanting to give to others that I chose to forgive. Choosing to forgive is not an option; it is a must! The word of God says that if we don't forgive, God will not forgive us (Mark 11:26, Matthew 6:15).

> But if ye do not forgive, neither will your Father which is in heaven forgive your trespasses. (Mark 11:26 KJV)

Having unforgiveness in your heart will keep you in bondage and hinders all that God wants to do in your life. Sometimes, we think that people are the hindrances but that is not always the case. I recall getting hurt by the words of a leader who was my spiritual mentor. When I went into prayer, crying out like we like to do, God revealed to me that the reason I was hurting was I was not walking in the Spirit. Imagine that, I was like what God. Yes, he repeated himself saying that if I was walking in the Spirit, the words that my mentor spoke would not have had an effect on me. My heart would have been guarded by the scriptures and his character. What am I saying? When people say or do things, if you are not walking in the Spirit it is going to hurt your flesh. When you can walk in the Spirit of God, you will be obedient to his word and take on his character and will speak like Jesus, when he said, "Father forgive them for they know not what they do." We have to stop looking at who is right and who is wrong. Jesus did not come to take sides.

As I talk to so many people, they have allowed unforgiveness to settle in their heart because of what someone has said or done or didn't say or do. The bottom line is, we must take on the character of God and do as my husband so often says, let it roll off you like Teflon. We can choose to let it stick, but if we do, the hurt turns into anger, anger turns into bitterness, bitterness turns into resentment, and resentment turns into unforgiveness. When God broke down what happened, of course he is the truth, I saw that unforgiveness is of the flesh, which is why it is important to conduct self-examination frequently. Jesus said that offenses will come. Having a spirit of forgiveness will help us to remain free, and open the doors for us to receive the promises of God. You don't ever have to worry about getting someone back for what has been done to you, vengeance will always be in the hands of God, if he so desires. We must remember that God loves us all, and he is not always wanting vengeance as we do; he desires relationship.

Forgiveness releases promises and causes us to grow and mature. The desire to be free and see others free is the love that God has for us all. Throughout the word of God, Jesus was constantly demonstrating the power of forgiveness. Forgiveness releases healing and restoration in your life and the lives of those that need forgiveness. As we forgive, we shouldn't do it grudgingly but whole-heartedly. You should never make your forgiveness conditional nor have an expectation of another person's response. I have heard people say oh, that person didn't forgive because if they did, they would have asked me to forgive them. That is not always the case, it is all about whether God speaks to that person and tells them to come back to the person to ask them for forgiveness. We must get away from pressing upon others how and what we would do, as if to say our way it is the only right way. Forgiveness doesn't bind, it looses! Forgiveness doesn't come with stipulations, control, or manipulations of others. It is done freely, at no charge, where you cast what has been done into the sea of forgetfulness.

You have heard, oh I can forgive but I can't forget. Yes, you can. God did it for you; he forgave you as far as the east is from the west. He could not have said in his word as far as the north is from the south. Why? Because the north and south have ending points, but the east and the west do not. That is a nugget that was revealed by the Holy Ghost. You must choose the way of the Lord over your mind, will and emotions.

Forgiveness allows you to move into your higher calling in Christ Jesus. You won't be effective in the ministry carrying around unforgiveness in your heart because hurt people will hurt people. We have to make up our minds to live "in" Christ versus living in a place of unforgiveness. There is no life in unforgiveness, and yes, unforgiveness can cause health issues.

Today, I refuse to allow unforgiveness to settle in my heart. Although I may have to shed some tears at times, my friend, the Holy Spirit knows how to comfort me. I have grown to realize that sometimes when people do things, it is not always on purpose. Sometimes, they are not aware of what they may have said or done, so release yourself and them. Don't take on vain imaginations. Cast them down because if you meditate on them long enough, unforgiveness won't be too far behind. Like everything in our lives, forgiveness is a choice, and when you choose to walk in forgiveness, you choose to walk in the power of Christ. You are free and you close the door of the enemy. Forgiveness is a gift. It requires a renewing of the mind to be willing to forgive over and over, because as long as you live in this life, you will experience life. And life comes with bumps and bruises. I pray that it is less than more, but remember when Peter asked Jesus, how many times do I have to forgive my brother or sister who has wronged or sinned against me, Jesus replied seventy times seven (Matthew 18:21). Once again, forgiveness is not an option, it is a must.

As you draw nigh unto God, ask him to reveal areas in your life where you may be carrying unforgiveness; then forgive. I encourage you to release yourself, and if you find it more challenging to do, be honest. Tell God and ask the Holy Spirit to help you. You must want to let it go because it will hinder you from having an intimate relationship with the Father, and more importantly, separate you from God eternally (Mark 11:26).

Drawing Nigh Chapter Challenge

Ask God to forgive you. Then, ask him for the grace to always be willing to forgive all those who have, or you perceive to have, wronged, maligned, persecuted, falsely accused, hurt, or abused you (spiritually, physically, mentally and verbally). Decide to live a life forgetting and pressing towards the high calling in Christ Jesus. Listen and obey the voice of the Holy Spirit. Guard your heart with the word of God and faith in God. Choose to live a life of casting down vain imaginations and drawing nigh unto God. Let nothing or no one interrupt or distract you from a relationship with God. It is easy when you choose to take Jesus' yoke. Remember, life is all about choices. God knows what you need when you need it. Pray and ask for wisdom and discernment because sometimes, it is not always what it seems, nor what you think or perceive.

Chapter 5: Deliverance is the Children's Bread

This chapter was by far the hardest to write and one that came with much warfare and resistance. It is a subject that has received so many negative connotations and there is nothing the enemy would desire more than to continue to keep God's children in the dark. But the still small voice whispered, who are you going to obey? The subject of deliverance is another book to be written all by itself and many authors have written on the subject.

My purpose is not to write on different types, methods, or the ministry of deliverance, but to expose you to the possibility of opening your heart as you draw nigh unto God for a deeper intimate relationship with him. I also wrote this chapter so that the enemy does not rob you of another great gift that God has for your life, which is the need for deliverance. I am writing to plant a seed that God can use another to water another, and so ultimately, God can bring an increase and deliverance to his children. I pray as you continue to read, that you would give your ears to the Holy Spirit and listen to what the Spirit of the Lord is saying. Will you hear?

What I mean by "Deliverance is the Children's Bread" is that because of the blood of Jesus, and his coming for all mankind, deliverance came to all. What is deliverance? Deliverance is merely an act of being rescued from a place of danger and bondage, free from the powers of Satan and the forces of evil. God is our deliverer, and because of his goodness and mercy he rescues us from evil, the evil one, dark places, and areas in our lives where we have opened the door for the enemy to reside. As we pray Matthew 6:11, "give us this day, our daily bread," asking for God's provision for our lives, spiritually, physically, and mentally against the wiles of the enemy, we must be free from all powers of the enemy. Deliverance is the washing and cleansing of the Holy Spirit moving in one's life. It is when the Holy Spirit allows areas of our life to surface so that we can repent, denounce, renounce, and ask forgiveness and forgive.

Deliverance was never meant to be frightening, but it is a blessing. Through deliverance we can be made whole and complete, loosed from the bonds of wickedness and evil, and set free from the works of our flesh, strongholds of lies, and deceit in our minds that have lead us into captivity. We have the truth of God's word, that we are overcomers and greater is he that is in us than he that is in the world (1 John 4:4), We are more than conquerors in Christ Jesus (Romans 8:37). But what happens when we encounter negativity, disappointments, hurt, pain, frustration, bitterness, and anger, or find ourselves in place that is against God's will, plan, and purpose for our lives? What do we do? How do we handle situations that overtake us? How do we stop the addictive habits in our lives? Knowing that we are overcomers in Christ, how do we overcome the areas of sin that confront us? How do we keep ourselves from what we call "small sins" or things we don't think of as sin like lying, gossiping, backbiting, deception, dishonesty, lack of integrity, and slander? These are things that we don't pay attention to in our lives because we focus more on "the larger sins," condemning the world of murdering, stealing, etc., drawing attention away from ourselves. The enemy is continuously planning evil against the children of God, and because of that we must know how to free ourselves from the enemy's power. We can take refuge in Psalms 91, but in the third verse, we are reminded of God's promise to be our deliver from the snares of the enemy.

> For it is He who delivers you from the snare of the trapper and from the deadly pestilence. (Psalm 91:3 NASB)

We thank God that he is our deliverer!

No one is exempt from deliverance. I am reminded of Paul when he wrote, "For sin, taking occasion by the commandment, deceived me, and by it slew me." (Romans 7:11 KJV) "For that which I do I allow not: for what I would, that do I not; but what I hate, that do I." (Romans 7:15 KJV)

> Now then it is no more I that do it, but sin that dwelleth in me.
>
> For I know that in me (that is, in my flesh,) dwelleth no good thing: for to will is present with me; but how to perform that which is good I find not. For the good that I would I do not: but the evil which I would not, that I do. Now if I do that I would not, it is no more I that do it, but sin that dwelleth in me. I find then a law, that, when I would do good, evil is present with me. For I delight in the law of God after the inward man: But I see another law in my members, warring against the law of my mind, and bringing me into **captivity to the law of sin** which is in my members. O wretched man that I am! **who shall deliver me** from the body of this death? (Romans 7:17-24 KJV emphasis added).

I believe Paul has said it best, and we must realize that *no one is exempt* from the need for deliverance in our lives. Contrary to our admittance, we all need deliverance from something. Sadly, the Body of Christ hides from the need for deliverance under the disguises of working for the Lord, positions, titles, gifts, and five-fold functions. We use these things as masks, but never allow God to deal with our heart and the deep areas of our lives that hinder us from a more intimate relationship with him. We prefer the appearance of godliness over the power of God.

In such a time as this, God is requiring his people to move us from a place of talking the talk, into a position of walking the walk. As we discussed in the first chapter of the book, it is only when we are honest with ourselves and willing to go through the process of self-examination that we can draw nigh unto God. Self-examination is where he can openly expose our hearts. I have had the privilege and honor of working and communicating with a diverse group of people, saved and unsaved, who are not aware that doors have been opened and the enemy has taken residence in areas of our lives. These open doors continue to result in ungodly and unruly behavior that is far from the character of God.

The time to act is now. God is yet revealing what is in our hearts, and the motives for our actions and reactions. In this world, we can witness the need for God our deliverer. Deliverance is not often spoken about because it requires truth, honesty, and transparency; henceforth, fewer people feel the need to be delivered, go through the washing and cleansing of deliverance, or have even heard of deliverance. When drawing nigh unto God, there is not an option to not open your heart. This is the reason God said to me, "Are you going to obey me?" in writing this chapter.

I know how seriously deliverance is needed because of what I see every day; watching the children of God struggle over and over, always in the wilderness, being stuck in the valley, and never able to go through. It brings sadness and grief to my heart. God has given us himself, not only to save us but to deliver us. Deliverance is the children's bread, and just because we receive salvation doesn't mean we have been totally delivered. Although, some deliverance can take place during the process of receiving the gift of salvation.

I can't continue without being transparent about my greatest life-changing experience and how, through it, God delivered me. After having a child out of wedlock, God healed my heart, hurt, pain, and brokenness. God peeled back the layers of my life at the age of thirty-two. The Holy Spirit began to reveal the excess weight that I was carrying, and things that I had not dealt with and didn't even know were there.

The enemy wants to keep us in darkness with the misconception that if God has healed us then we are okay, and we don't need deliverance. However, you must know that there is a difference in being healed and receiving deliverance. You can be healed but not have deliverance. That is why you must draw nigh unto God and continue in the process of self-examination.

You say, "But why?" That is your question for God. But let me explain how God gave me revelation and insight into the two parts of being whole and complete in Him. The process of being whole came through the healing of the hurt, pain, shame, and guilt where God filled the empty voids. The completion process came through the deliverance from the sin of sexual immorality, the breaking of soul-ties that binds one to another person through the act of sin. Are you following me? There was deliverance from the evil and darkness of the sin, and the strongholds of Satan's lies and deceit that tortured my mind. There was freedom from the accuser of the brethren, and deliverance from the bondages and captivities of Satan's power. For me, the healing took place first, and soon thereafter the deliverance process began. I give glory to God when I think of the goodness of God and all that he has done for me! We must be free from all powers of the enemy.

Deliverance requires obedience and submission to God's will for your life. I am a witness that the process of deliverance is seasoned with God's love and grace. His love and grace kept me close to him as he would minister to me through the power of the Holy Ghost. I can recall him saying, "Marilyn, it was not that having a child was not in my plans for your life." It was just that I had skipped chapters and now needed to go through the process of washing and cleansing so that God could bring me back in line to the story that he had written about me.

He was writing my story just like so many of us today. Deliverance will delete chapters that are not of God from our lives. When I hear people sing the song *You Don't Know My Story*, and tears begin to fall from my eyes, I can discern if they have been healed or delivered or both. God began to speak to me about the sound of deliverance. "Marilyn," he would say, "Listen to the sound that is coming forth." There is a different sound of deliverance that proceeds from a person when he or she is speaking. Deliverance comes with a sound of joy, peace, gratefulness, thankfulness, and excitement. In contrast, the need for deliverance comes with a sound of anger, bitterness, yelling, and screaming to name a few. It can come forward whenever I am listening to someone speaking, preaching, or teaching.

Deliverance is performed through the power of the Holy Ghost, not through the person that may be taking you through the process. Pray and seek God and he will lead you to the right person. During the process, the Holy Spirit is the examiner. As I said before, this chapter was to bring you into awareness for an open heart. I can't say how God will deliver you, but I can say that you must want to be delivered. It is easy to put on a mask, and the truth is that we can start off wearing one mask, but if we don't confront areas in our lives, other masks are formed. Before we know it, we have a mask to wear with every outfit. We keep the masks, and act as if we have it all together, but each time we allow the stronghold to become stronger. In this journey called life, we have all been a product of "damaged goods" (another book to be released at another time). It doesn't matter who we are; no one is exempt.

Deliverance is a process and not everyone's process is the same. Some people's deliverance may come instantly, for some it may happen in a day, and for some, it may happen in weeks, months, or years. It is a repetitive process. Did I just say *repetitive* process? Yes, because we live in this world and go through life. We encounter things and things happen to us, so deliverance is not a one-time thing. Therefore, drawing nigh to God through self-examination should take place often in our lives.

Deliverance is also the timing of God. He may expose areas in our lives at different times. Some people have suppressed their issues and healing may have to come first to be able to endure the deliverance process. To this day, the Holy Spirit will reveal to me when and where I have opened a door and need to be delivered. Yes, I have gone through deliverance sessions, and at the time the Holy Spirit does it himself. But don't be ignorant of Satan's devices, schemes, tactics, and lies to believe that it is something that you can do by yourself.

Remember, my purpose was not to go through the different types or methods of deliverance, but to expose you to the possibility of opening your heart as you draw nigh unto God for a deeper, intimate relationship with him. I pray that the enemy does not rob you of another great gift that God has for your life and that a seed has been planted. The truth is that salvation is free but there is a cost that goes with the truth, which is the cost of change. There is freedom and liberty that you haven't experienced yet until you have been delivered! I want to encourage you to give God thanks and receive all the benefits of God. As we pray give us this day, our daily bread, know that deliverance is one of our provisions against the wiles of the enemy.

Drawing Nigh Chapter Challenge

As you draw nigh unto God, knowing that he loves you, ask the Holy Spirit to reveal to you any area(s) that may be holding you captive or in bondage. Ask him to show you where deliverance needs to take place. Also, seek to be healed from all hurt, pain, or brokenness in your heart. Begin searching the word of God and studying the scriptures about God as your deliverer. Speak to your pastor or ask the Holy Spirit to lead and guide you to someone who understands deliverance. Remember, no one is exempt from the need to be delivered. Deliverance is part of us being perfected (our growth) so that we can become more like Jesus and produce more fruit.

Chapter 6: Religion versus Relationship

There are many evil spirits that come to hinder the believer and work against the building of God's Kingdom. The one we address in this chapter is the spirit of religion. It is infiltrating the body of Christ. And we can see its work in a greater division and disunity. The spirit of religion is dangerous because it causes havoc, destroys relationships, takes on a form of godliness, and brings confusion and devastation in the lives of people. The spirit of religion seeks to keep believers carnal-minded, self-righteous, judgmental, and prejudice towards each other.

Religion, in simple terms, can be defined as a personal set or institutionalized system of attitudes, beliefs, and practice. Religion can influence one's behavior and actions and how they respond to God and the people of God. Religion stems from man's ideology, thoughts, ideas, and culture. We are seeing more and more conformation to religion in the body of Christ and less and less transformation by the working of the Holy Spirit.

There is a danger that has crept into the household of faith, and people are exalting their own knowledge and will against the knowledge and will of God. It can happen subtly when persuasion and the influence of man is for any purpose other than the will of God and what he wants to accomplish. It can also happen when we do not allow the power of the Holy Spirit to lead and guide in all things concerning the people of God and the work of the ministry, and when man's agenda becomes greater than God. Today, we see some cases where the relationship between man (each other) has become more important than a relationship with the Father. God desires for his children to have their own personal relationship with him, and that they strive each day for that relationship to become more and more intimate.

In the Bible, Jesus dealt with religious people, the scribes, and Pharisees. They were the people that had the responsibility to teach the word of God, but somehow got off track (which is what has happened today). In Matthew chapter twenty-three, Jesus dealt harshly with those in leadership because of their responsibility to the people. Jesus instructed his disciples that they were not to do the works of the Scribes and Pharisees. Please read Matthew chapter twenty-three. There you see religious spirits at work.

Religious spirits take on the form of self-righteous, self-indignation, judgmental, arrogance, and pride. Religion, operating through religious spirits, wants others to conform to their ideas, thoughts, and how they see and view a subject or situation. Religion tells people how they should act and what they should be doing. And it takes precedence over what God's word says or uses God's word out of context. That is why it is so important to walk in a spirit of humility; be willing and open to self-examination. Repent, forgive, and ask God to deliver you from self-will so that as a Christian, you do not allow the spirit of religion to creep in.

The spirit of religion does not take hold overnight. It creeps its way into a person's heart and will give an open door to what is called a religious spirit. We all are at risk for being influenced by and operating through a religious spirit at some point in our lives if we are honest. And you will see it as I begin to expose the actions of a religious spirit. Religious spirits operate from a place of self, and you will see it more so when the works of a person are exalted above others. God desires a relationship more than your gifts and works; besides, all that we have and do came from him.

There is to be a balance in the work of the ministry for the kingdom of God. God has an established order and structure for the body of Christ. A relationship with him first takes priority in order to carry out his will. Because so much focus has been on "work," many times we find ourselves striving to do more work versus seeking a relationship. Don't get me wrong, the work of the ministry is important to the kingdom, but it is not to replace or substitute a relationship with the Father.

I learned that doing the work of the ministry doesn't mean that you have a relationship with the God. I will never forget when I had become so heavily involved in my duties in the church. I fell into the religious spirit's trap of believing if you don't do this or that, then you don't love God. If you don't do this or that, you are walking in disobedience and rebellion; you are not submitting. I didn't say no to some of the work that I knew I should have said no to because I wanted to do what was asked of me. I can't blame anyone but myself. I had become void in areas of my life where I used to be filled.

I will never forget a life-changing experience I had one Saturday morning. I was sitting on my back porch, listening to worship music, and tears begin to fall. Suddenly, out of my spirit I cried, "God, I am doing all this, yet I feel so lonely." The Holy Spirit whispered, "Marilyn, where you once were, you are no longer." I was puzzled. He went on to speak, "You left your position, and now you are in a place. You were once positioned in me, now it is just a place of doing." The Holy Spirit reminded me of the times when I was positioned in God's presence, where we communed together. That is the position that fills and satisfies. I left my position to a place of working. I was so busy preparing for God to move, that I moved in the process.

We must always seek to be like Mary—at the feet of Jesus first. Then we take on the role of Martha. If done in that order, we won't get tired, murmur, complain, or worry about what someone else is doing.

> As Jesus and his disciples were on their way, he came to a village where a woman named Martha opened her home to him. She had a sister called Mary, who sat at the Lord's feet listening to what he said. But Martha was distracted by all the preparations that had to be made. She came to him and asked, "Lord, don't you care that my sister has left me to do the work by myself? Tell her to help me!" Martha, Martha," the Lord answered, "you are worried and upset about many things, but few things are needed—or indeed only one.[a] Mary has chosen what is better, and it will not be taken away from her. (Luke 10: 38-42 KJV)

In John 5:19 and John 12:49, Jesus said that he only does and speaks what the Father tells him to do and speak. Likewise, we should always seek God for his will and allow the Holy Spirit to rule our lives and the body of Christ. There is an unseen danger to religion that has crept into the body of Christ. It is robbing people from a true relationship with the Father and moving them more toward a relationship and dependency on man. As I refer to man throughout this book, it is not in reference to gender but mankind, male and female. This happens most often when we are seeking the approval of man instead of the approval of God; when a person puts their agenda above the agenda and purpose of God. A religious spirit values and focuses on titles and positions and seeks to rise above and outdo another. It exalts itself and thinks of itself more highly than it ought. As a result, we see the people of God focusing more on seeking positions and titles rather than a relationship with God. As Christians, we must know that we are positioned and seated in a great place with Christ, and we have been given the title of sons and daughters of El Elyon, the most high God! Let us realize that God sent forth Jesus because he is desiring sonship.

When God spoke to me about this chapter, the Holy Spirit had me look back to a time in my life when I was attacked by religious spirits. I too was tricked and had fallen prey to religious spirits. In 2019, when God sent my husband and I out to establish a place of worship, we couldn't just go. Oh yes, we tried, but we were both in prayer. My husband and I shared what God was saying to us in our prayer times. God was saying to the both of us that before we began to build, there was a reconstruction that he needed to do in our lives first. There was a foundation that he needed to lay, not from the perspective of what we had come to know through watching others, but his desires for what he was calling us to do.

The more we tuned in to him, the more he spoke concerning relationship, the core of his heart for his people. He showed us what was becoming our first and foremost desire, and what we realized had taken second place at times throughout the years of doing the work of the ministry. As God continued to reveal, we surrendered, yielded, and made up our minds that we would not move, but allow God to rebuild, remold, reshape, and renew our mindsets. We often laugh because we were still being faced with religious spirits trying to woo us back into the old ways of thinking, tradition, and religion.

Each week, the Holy Spirit begin to share insight and enlighten us on the importance of the kingdom, the ministry of Jesus, and allowing God to deal with our hearts. Only then would the manifestation of the assignment come forth in fullness, glory, and the beauty of God's will, purpose, and plans. God would establish it! The more we prayed and dived into the word of God, the more our lives begin to transform. Both my husband and I have been in ministry for over twenty-five years, and some would say, that is a long time. But in hindsight, let me say it was also a long time for religious spirits to take root. Today, we are both so grateful to God as we had to walk out every chapter of this book, allowing God to wash, cleanse, and purify our hearts. Thank you, God.

Understanding your Relationship with the Father as Leaders and Disciples

God sets leaders (apostles, prophets, evangelist, pastors, and teachers, whatever the title may be) in the house to watch over the souls of his people. They are the set leaders of the house; they are the ones to whom God speaks the vision and mandate of the house. They are accountable to God for what takes place in their lives and in the house of God. Their love for Jesus operates through feeding and not scattering the sheep. They teach, train, and equip the disciples (not members) of God to go out into the uttermost parts of the earth preaching the gospel of the kingdom. They have the great responsibility to ensure the work of the ministry is carried out. They establish the foundation based on the word of God and they ensure the ministry is ruled, governed, and operates by and through the Spirit of God—the Holy Spirit only. They should understand the importance of seeking unity and oneness of the Spirit—the Spirit of God; they should walk in humility and love at all times!

God set disciples (not members) in the house of God to be taught, trained, and equipped to grow and mature in the things of God. Disciples are to work together as members, as in the illustration of Paul, as bodily members, needing each other to carry out the work of the ministry for the kingdom of God to rule on earth. Disciples discipline themselves to be taught the word of God to go out into the uttermost parts of the earth preaching the Gospel of the kingdom. Disciples understand that they are under the authority of the set leader; henceforth, shall be submissive and obey their leaders. Disciples too are accountable to God for what takes place in their lives and in the house of God. They understand their role to help and give themselves to be led of the spirit of God, the Holy Spirit. Disciples seek unity and oneness of the Spirit—the Spirit of God; they should walk in humility and love at all times!

Acts of Religious Spirits Contrary to a Relationship with the Father

Religious spirits are all about the outward appearance and self-gratification. They always speak of themselves. They want others to know and see what they are doing. "I" is the center of the conversation. I did this, or look at what I am doing. "I" prayed for "x" amount of hours; "I" am fasting. A religious spirit causes one to honor oneself. The list goes on and on, but just remember, "I" will always be the center. A right spirit focuses on a relationship with the Father, seeks the Father's will, and does not bring attention to oneself nor take the glory away from God. Whatever is done is to the glory of the Father. A right spirit does not pray openly to be heard, give openly to be seen, or speak of what they do. Whatever is done, is done in secret relationship because of the love for the Father. A relationship with God acknowledges God, and honors God as well as God in others.

A religious spirit rules from a place of spiritual abuse, disrespect, and dictatorial power not from the authority given by God. A religious spirit often speaks condemnation. It releases and speaks word curses on the people of God. A religious spirit lacks kindness, is harsh, and unhelpful. A relationship with the Father loves despite any wrongdoing. Relationship rules from a place of gentleness and kindness. A relationship seeks to encourage and build up, is motivated by love, and corrects by love. Understand that God doesn't call his children negative names and such name calling is a form of witchcraft. Relationship with the Father quickens one to speak life knowing that life and death is in the power of the tongue. A relationship seeks to pray for the weaker vessel and is helpful, when they see someone stumble their desire is to restore.

A religious spirit wants ownership of the people of God. It operates through control and manipulation. Religious spirits seek the position of God and the Holy Spirit in a person's life. A right spirit in relationship with the Father:

- understands that the people belong to God;

- the role they have been given has been entrusted by God;

- is not dictatorial, but leads by example;

- is a follower of Christ through the working of the Holy Spirit;

- knows that the same spirit that raised Jesus from the dead lives inside everyone; and,

- encourages others to seek God.

A religious spirit places people in bondage by manipulating them to conform to man's desires, ideas, rules, and standards. It creates a culture of fear and restricts the movement of God. A right spirit focused on relationship with the Father speaks and allows the freedom and liberty of God to move in the lives of God's people. It teaches what Jesus taught, said, and did; it encourages the following of Christ. A right spirit focused on relationship with God allows the Holy Spirit to operate and releases blessings into the lives of God's people.

Religious spirits judge through outward appearances, through the natural eye. Relationship understands that no man knows the heart of man, and God works in a person's life from the inside out.

A religious spirit tears down, brings division, isolation, and separation in the hearts of the people and the body of Christ. A relationship with the Father builds up, edifies, exalts, upholds integrity, and works in unity and harmony with the same Spirit (Holy Spirit). A right spirit focused on relationship with God understands that no one denomination has a monopoly on God; we all operate in part. As it is written in James 4:11 NLT, "Don't speak evil against each other, dear brothers and sisters. If you criticize and judge each other, then you are criticizing and judging God's law. But your job is to obey the law, not to judge whether it applies to you." Relationship with God does not speak evil against one another.

Religious spirits bring condemnation, make people feel guilty or ashamed. Relationship with the Father rebuilds, restores, understands the children of God are in Christ Jesus, and teaches the children of God to walk not after the flesh, but after the Spirit. It operates through the blood of Jesus and understands that it was only Jesus who died for the sins of the world.

Religious spirits set-up and operate through man's by-laws. Relationship with the Father confirms we are no longer under the law. According to Romans 10:4 NIV, " Christ is the culmination of the law so that there may be righteousness for everyone who believes."

Religious spirits reject people because of their social economic status, race, gender, and what they do or don't do. A relationship with the Father has no respect of persons, and is accepting of all because of the love of God. Religious spirits operate through false perceptions, distorted views, and are influence by self. Religious spirits are man's thoughts, ideologies, traits, and characteristics.

Because we want to speak our opinions, we are all susceptible to allowing religious spirits to operate in our lives. We must begin not only to go to church but also become the church. We must not only listen to the word of God, but also study and apply the word of God. It is the word of God that transforms us into being like Christ. In 2 Timothy 2:15, the word tells us to study to show ourselves approved unto God, so that we won't be ashamed. But we will be able to divide the truth from any spirit that is not of God. We must be extremely careful and always sensitive to the Spirit of God. We must first and foremost value what God's desire is for our lives and each other. And if you are a leader, you have a great responsibility to not fall into the traps of religious spirits. You have been placed in a position of authority and entrusted by God to care for his people.

Drawing Nigh Chapter Challenge

For this chapter, I challenge you to stop and look at your life. How are you viewing other? Do you see them in the image of God? Or are you more focused on getting them to adhere to your standards and desires? Ask yourself whether you are focused on building your relationship with the Father or spending more time doing the work of the ministry or neither. What is first and foremost in your heart and in your walk with God. What does your relationship with the Father look like? Do you know God or know "of" God? Are you in a place or position? If you don't know the simplest thing to do is to ask God!

Chapter 7: Strengthening our Relationship with the Father

I am glad that you are yet reading this book. The next few chapters are to encourage you. No matter who you are and where you are in your life, as you draw nigh unto God, you will know the depth of his love for you. As I continue in prayer, the Holy Spirit bought back to my remembrance the importance of a relationship with our Heavenly Father and that it is God's desire today for his children. I am a testimony, that a relationship with God is one of the most joyous and peaceful times of my life as I walk with him. It is through a relationship that we come to know our Father. Every believer has a responsibility to grow in their relationship with the Father, and make it personal where it is just you and your God. The blessed assurance is that even though no two people's relationship will be the same, the principles of God's word will be the same.

As a believer, you should never compare your relationship to another person. Each of us must develop our own personal relationship with him. God does not want you to beat yourself up thinking that you don't measure up for whatever reason. God just wants you to respond to him. To get a better understanding of a relationship, think about some of your current relationships. What makes a good relationship? What makes a bad relationship? In every relationship, someone must initiate it first, and thereafter, it takes both people for the relationship to grow and flourish.

A relationship is defined as a connection between two or more people. In this case the two or more is, God the Father, Jesus the Son, Holy Ghost, and the believer. A relationship requires work from both parties, the believer and God. A relationship is also defined as the way in which two or more people regard and behave toward each other; and it is an affair of the heart. So a relationship begins within our hearts, and our desire for God's will and purpose for our lives. Our *love* for God should drive a relationship with him. It is not the work of the ministry, our church attendance, titles, position, gifts, nor talents. It is not just works. If we are not careful, we can easily flow over into the works of the flesh. Our hearts must be pure; our desire must be for God himself and not what God can do for us. We should be seeking his face and not his hands. In the fast paste of this world, it is so easy to get caught up in its systems, mode of thinking, and behavior pattern where God becomes last when he should be first. We take the time to focus on relationships with our family, friends, boyfriends, girlfriends, and other areas of our life. Henceforth, we should spend even more time on our relationship with God. Matthew 6: 33-34 KJV says, "But seek ye first the kingdom of God, and his righteousness; and all these things shall be added unto you. Take therefore no thought for the morrow: for the morrow shall take thought for the things of itself. Sufficient unto the day is the evil thereof." There is a lot going on in the world, I want to encourage you to draw nigh unto God. Being in a relationship with the Father, is what will keep us, especially during life struggles, trials, and circumstances. Because we know who we are connected to, and that we have a God that is yet in control we can overcome. Our relationship with God keeps us in position and grounded in him. We won't lose our love, joy, and peace, and we are able to bear much fruit. I want to encourage you to make your relationship with him more secure and deeper than ever before. God has so much he wants to get to you and through you. He will take care of you and everything that concerns you, but you will never know that if you don't develop a relationship with Him.

Jesus was the initiator. Our relationship with the Father began when we believed in our heart and confessed with our mouth. Then, we were saved. Romans 10:10 NIV says, "For it is with your heart that you believe and are justified, and it is with your mouth that you profess your faith and are saved. When Jesus died on the cross for us, we were simultaneously justified, redeemed, and reconciled back to the Father. That brought us back into a relationship with the Father.

It is deeper and this is what the Holy Spirit began to speak to me concerning God's desire for his children to draw nigh unto him. I will never forget when he enlightened me that a believer can be saved and still not have a relationship with God. I thought, but when Jesus died on the cross, didn't he bring us back to a relationship with God? He reconciled us and redeemed us. But as God spoke and I listened, he spoke in a parable to explain what he meant.

It was a revelation and transformation that changed my life completely. He explained it to me this way. Jesus made the way; he initiated a relationship for us, but *to have* a relationship goes a little further than the believer's salvation. The script was flipped as he spoke for me to ponder this. You see, with someone you love, you go to them and say, hello, I want you to know that I love you more than you will ever know and there is nothing that I won't do for you. There is nothing that you have to do but only say "yes." I will give you your every heart's desire. Will you marry me? The other person says yes, with so much excitement, and you get married. The next day, you begin to talk to your new found love. Now, the person doesn't respond. Repeatedly, you keep calling and do all you can to get their attention. There's little response; nothing that shows love. You nudge them, and nothing happens. You give them good gifts, you are always there, you listen to them when they come to talk; but as you begin to talk, they get up and walk away. You continue to speak, and sometimes there is a response. You tell them what is best for them, and they obey sometimes. You give everything, and they sometimes remember to say thank you. This goes on for weeks and months, and soon years go by. You are doing all you can to get their attention, but it only happens when the other person feels like it. You constantly tell them and send messages through others to let them know that you love them, and nothing they do ever changes. I think you get the picture.

Now, based on what we know a relationship to be, would you say that there is a relationship between those two people? Do you see where one is the giver and one is the receiver? Would you want to be in a relationship like that? Sadly, for some people that is what their relationship is like with God and other people. Isaiah 54:5 tells us that God, our maker, is our husband. In Ephesians 5, Jesus used the illustration of a marriage between a husband and wife to symbolize what our relationship with the Father should be. We are the bride of Christ; Jesus is married to the church. Satan attacks marriages because of it is symbolic of the union of God and the believer in relationship. We must not be ignorant of the enemy; he comes to destroy our relationship with God. That is why it can be hard for some people who have been in a bad relationship to understand the goodness of a relationship with the Father. Although, there was not a cost to us for the gift of salvation, there was a price that had to be paid. And the price came with a purpose, which is a relationship with our heavenly Father. We have been redeemed by the blood of Jesus for the purpose of knowing God. The only way to know our Father is to build a relationship with him. It was through knowing that I was redeemed and reconciled that I was led to my relationship with God and restored.

Jesus's Redemptive Power

Ephesians 1:7-14 was a life changer. It says:

> In him we have redemption through his blood, the forgiveness of sins, in accordance with the riches of God's grace that he lavished on us. With all wisdom and understanding, he made known to us the mystery of his will according to his good pleasure, which he purposed in Christ, to be put into effect when the times reach their fulfillment-to bring unity to all things in heaven and on earth under Christ. In him we were also chosen, having been predestined according to the plan of him who works out everything in conformity with the purpose of his will, in order that we, who were the first to put our hope in Christ, might be for the praise of his glory. And you also were included in Christ when you heard the message of truth, the gospel of your salvation. When you believed, you were marked in him with a seal, the promised Holy Spirit, who is a deposit guaranteeing our inheritance until the redemption of those who are God's

possession—to the praise of his glory. (Ephesians 1:7-14 NIV)

Jesus Ministry of Reconciliation

Knowing, therefore, the terror of the Lord, we persuade men; but we are well known to God, and I also trust are well known in your consciences. For we do not commend ourselves again to you, but give you opportunity to boast on our behalf, that you may have an answer for those who boast in appearance and not in heart. For if we are beside ourselves, it is for God; or if we are of sound mind, it is for you. For the love of Christ compels us, because we judge thus: that if One died for all, then all died; and He died for all, that those who live should live no longer for themselves, but for Him who died for them and rose again. Therefore, from now on, we regard no one according to the flesh. Even though we have known Christ according to the flesh, yet now we know Him thus no longer. Therefore, if anyone is in Christ, he is a new creation; old things have passed away; behold, all things have become new. Now all things are of God, who has reconciled us to Himself through Jesus Christ, and has given us the ministry of reconciliation, that is, that God was in Christ reconciling the world to Himself, not imputing their trespasses to them, and has committed to us the word of reconciliation. Now then, we are ambassadors for Christ, as though God were pleading through us: we implore you on Christ's behalf, be reconciled to God. For He made Him who knew no sin to be sin for us, that we might become the righteousness of God in Him. (2 Corinthians 5:11-21 NKJV)

Drawing Nigh Chapter Challenge

I challenge you to decide to get to know your God through a relationship with him. I challenge you to read and study Ephesians 1:7-14 and 2 Corinthians 5:11-21. Remember that your Christian walk requires a relationship that is only between you and your God. There is so much that God wants to reveal to you concerning your purpose. There are conversations that can only be had between you and him. Draw nigh and don't look back!

Chapter 8: God's Purpose for a Relationship

It is important to understand that our need for a relationship with God is so that we can understand who we are and who he is. 2 Corinthians 5:17 talks about us being new creatures, old things passing away, and all things becoming new. When we speak about salvation, it is not easy to comprehend. All most people can comprehend is Jesus dying on the cross for our sins because it was seen by man's natural eyes. When we speak about being a new creature, it is supernatural because it is something that you can't see. It is something you have to live out, and the only way to live out what is supernatural is to have the supernatural being himself give you revelation. Allowing him to reveal the new creature that we are is the beginning of our relationship with the Father. As we draw nigh unto God, his desire is for us to see ourselves in his image. During prayer as I was declaring this scripture, I begin to think about being made in the image of the Almighty, the creator of all things, and I thought, "Wow! It was above my comprehension. Then, as I begin to ponder, I heard the Holy Spirit whisper, "That is why we struggle, because we don't understand what it means to be a new creature." I reflected back to when I was first told that I was a new creature. I didn't understand, but I continued. I was reminded that often what we don't understand, we have a tendency to avoid, and before long, those things go unchecked. We move on, yet we never understand the fullness of who we are and the purpose of our salvation. We don't understand why God drew us to himself.

We were created in him for a relationship with him.

God wants to reveal to us who we are in him. God is a spirit, and we are created in the image of the God. But how will we know and understand the things of God except by having a relationship with him? We wouldn't want anyone to speak about who we are if we had not had some type of communication with them. Sadly, that is what is happening. We tend to believe that we truly know a person based off what we read about them. Granted, you may know some of the characteristics of a person from what you read about them (and some of us get that wrong). But for the person to share with you who they are requires a relationship. Likewise, God requires a relationship so that he can reveal who he is. Since God is a Spirit, it requires the Holy Spirit to give us revelation. That is why I said earlier that some people know of him but do not know him. Knowing him will cause transformation to take place in your heart, and God is all about dealing with what is in our heart. In 2 Corinthians 5: 18, Paul implores us on Christ's behalf to be reconciled to God and become the righteous of God in him. The way to understand the righteous of God is by getting to know who he is, which requires a relationship.

The Purpose of a Relationship with God

The purpose of a relationship with God is for us to know that we were created with purpose for a purpose. When God created you, he uniquely designed you for him and his good pleasure so that he will be glorified. Likewise, the Holy Spirit was given to us for purpose. While we each have a different purpose, all our purposes working together in unity (for the purpose of God) brings harmony. And unity in the body of Christ advances the kingdom of God and brings him glory. Our gifts, talents, and abilities are given according to our purpose. Therefore, in our relationship with God, he brings it all together for his good. The gifts of God should all work together for the purpose of God with the same Spirit, the Holy Spirit. When we don't know our purpose, we find ourselves trying to mimic someone else's ministry, works, gifts, and talents.

I hear so often that ministry is tiresome. It should not be when you are in relationship because just like Jesus, you are only doing what the Father tells you to do. Matthew 11:28 – 30 KJV says:

> Come unto me, all ye that labour and are heavy laden, and I will give you rest. Take my yoke upon you and learn of me; for I am meek and lowly in heart: and ye shall find rest unto your souls. For my yoke is easy, and my burden is light.

That is why a relationship with God is so important. You must *come* to God for your purpose to be fulfilled. In 2019, God launched my husband and I into ministry for an entire year. Yet today, he said, "Sit because transformation had to take place from what you have seen to what I have called you to do." We had to hop on the potter's wheel because there was molding and shaping that had to take place to shift from what we had seen, what we knew and thought, and mostly from our plans. Letting go was *not* an option. It has been the best year of our lives to be positioned by God for our purpose in him to be fulfilled.

I encourage you not to be a duplicator; seek God for your purpose. The world is waiting for the manifestation of the sons and daughters of God. Your relationship with God will bring stability to your purpose, and your purpose in him will be easy! Remember, God instructs us not to compare ourselves to anyone. Romans 12:6 MSG says, "let's just go ahead and be what we were made to be, without enviously or pridefully comparing ourselves with each other, or trying to be something we aren't." There is danger in trying to do something that you have not been created to do; it opens doors for the enemy to bring deception and distractions to get us off track. Always remember, it is not about your work for God but your relationship with him. We need God's instructions and will in everything we do. A relationship with the Father keeps us on the path of righteousness for his name sake. When God told Nehemiah to build the wall (Nehemiah 1), each time one assignment was complete, Nehemiah kept coming to receive more instructions for the next assignment. When God has spoken to us concerning our purpose, we must keep coming back to him to instruct and lead us. God fulfills his purpose through us, not we ourselves.

Coming into a Relationship – Our Helper, The Word, Prayer, and Obedience

God's love is unconditional, but there are conditions in our life. There are things that God will require us *to do* so that we *can become* more like Jesus. The purpose of this chapter is to share some key principles of God that are essential for coming into a relationship with the Father. They are principles that are not to be ignored. God desires is to give us his own heart. The Holy Spirit gives clarity, comprehension, and helps us to understand the Father. God has not changed. Just as he came through Christ, he now comes through the power of the Holy Spirit to reveal himself to us and tell us who we are so that we can become more like Christ.

We need our helper, the Holy Spirit; we cannot ignore him. He is the only one that can reveal the heart of God to us which should be every believer's desire. He is the only one that knows the Spirit of the Father. Although you gain teaching and equipping from the five-fold ministry, the Holy Spirit will enlighten you, give insight, and revelation of the word of God and the Father's will. He is our advocate and teacher. He aides us in our purpose, gifts, and talents and gives us power to do so. In John 16, Jesus said that it was to our benefit that He go away but that the advocate, the Holy Spirit, would come and he will guide us in all truth. He will speak what he hears from the Father, show us what is to come, and be our comforter. In the Old Testament, the Holy Spirit fell on the people of God. But in the New Testament, the Holy Spirit fell and they were filled with the Holy Spirit. Today, as believers and new creatures in Christ, we too are filled with the Holy Spirit. He resides on the inside of us. It is by the working of the power of the Holy Spirit that we fulfill the purpose of God in our lives (Romans 8:11).

We must read God's word.

As we come into a relationship with the Father, reading God's word is where we show our love and interest in him. In sincerity of heart for wanting to know him, we dig into the word to know who he is. Read 2 Timothy 2:15. It says, "Study to shew thyself approved unto God, a workman that needeth not to be ashamed, rightly dividing the word of truth." When we read and study the word of God, we should consult our helper, the Holy Spirit, for understanding. It is so easy to take on the world's definition of a word and apply it to the context of God's word. The word of God *cannot be defined* by Webster, Miriam, Wiki page, or any other accessible gadgets that have become resources in other areas of our lives. Though they have their purposes, revelation of the word is not one of them. 2 Peter 1:20-21 says, "Knowing this first, that no prophecy of the scripture is of any private interpretation. For the prophecy came not in old time by the will of man: but holy men of God spake as they were moved by the Holy Ghost." The Holy Spirit is our source, without Him the word is incomprehensible.

The word of God was given to help us know our heavenly Father, to give us examples, and teach and train us in every area of our being and existence. It was written as a guiding light to be the lamp unto our feet and a light unto our paths. The word of God is our weapon against the wiles of the devil; we must use the word just like Jesus did when the devil came to him. We cannot take authority over the enemy or any force of darkness without the word of God. Our victory and authority is in the word of God. The Holy Spirit will bring back to your remembrance the word that you are to release.

Coming into relationship with God is clearer, and we will find the reasons and understanding for a relationship and purposes when we read John 1:1, John 10:35b and Hebrews 4:12. John 1:1 lets us know God's will from the beginning was for us to be in relationship with him. It says, "In the beginning was the Word, and the Word was with God, and the Word was God." In John 10:35b, we see that God's word cannot be broken; it's everlasting and imperishable. In Hebrews 4:12, we see the word at work. It says, "For the word of God is quick, and powerful, and sharper than any two-edged sword, piercing even to the dividing asunder of soul and spirit, and of the joints and marrow, and is a discerner of the thoughts and intents of the heart." In Revelation 22:18-19, we see the danger of adding to and taking away from the word of God. When words are added to the scriptures, it makes God of no effect. When certain words are taken away, you are robbing God of who he is. Both can hurt the body of Christ. That is why when I hear the term "God said," I consult the Holy Spirit for the truth. Saying "God said" has become a way to control and manipulate God's people.

We must pray and cry out to God.

In our relationship with the Father, we must know that God's doors are always open, and his arms are always outstretched towards us. We do not have to be afraid. Although, he is almighty, and we are to reverence him and honor him because of who he is. We are to humble ourselves before him but not from a fearful and timid spirit. God wants you to know that he takes pleasure in you. That is reflected in how he has adorned us with his salvation (Genesis 1:1 and Psalms 149:4). God did not create us to have a spirit of fear (2 Timothy 1:7a). Isaiah 43:1 tells us not to fear but to know that God has redeemed us through Jesus Christ and called each of us by name. I speak to people that have backslidden or are unsaved, and most of the time they have been negatively impacted by something a believer has said. Typically, a believer had said something through a form of tradition and religion and opened the door for the enemy to cause havoc and cast lies and deceit to the person. That is why it is necessary that I give you scriptures in this book instead of opinions. There is nothing more grieving than a child of God who comes to church and is made to feel guilty, ashamed, and condemned. I have watched it happen time and time again. This is what blocks relationship between God and his people. God is concerned about the hindrances to a relationship with his children.

As you enter in his presence, you always want to honor God, but you do not have to be afraid to come to your Father. Remember, this book was birthed through prayer. I was not doing anything great. As a matter of fact, it wasn't my specific time of the day that I pray. I was drawn to prayer by God because he knew my thoughts. Remember, God knows our hearts; he searches our hearts. He purposely drew me by his Spirit for this purpose. My spirit was grieved by everything that was happening in the world. I had just listened to another senseless murder—a premature death of one of God's children. As children of God, we must get out of the habit of separating ourselves from humanity's hurts. Whether a person is saved or unsaved, we all belong to God. He is concerned if any of his children are lost. Remember, Jesus leaves the ninety-nine to go after the one that is lost (Matthew 18:12, Luke 15:4). We don't want to be like the religious leaders, with their self-righteous behavior and their rules and laws that were made to exclude and belittle those who didn't measure up to their standards. I am so grateful that I was the one that Jesus came after.

Whether you're starting a relationship or you've have had a relationship with him for many years, it should always be a continuous, ongoing lifestyle to draw nigh to God in prayer. I am not about to tell you how to pray, what you should say, or when to pray. I will leave that for the working of the Holy Spirit as God reveals. And it is never about the quantity or length of your prayers; it is about the quality and effectiveness of your prayers. I do want to encourage you. As you are in his presence, allow God an opportunity to speak to you as well. Hearing his voice directly or through the Holy Spirit is an awesome experience. Prayer can never be one-sided. If you have been the one that has been doing all the talking, you must begin to sit still. It may feel awkward at first, and without a doubt, the enemy will try to bombard your thoughts to distract you. If it helps, put on some instrumental worship music, but give your ear to the Holy Spirit. As you continue in prayer, your relationship will grow and deepen, and you will become more sensitive to the Holy Spirit. As it is in the natural, likewise it is in the Spirit; in communication we must listen as well as speak, giving an ear to hear what the receiver (God) has to say as well. It is your time with your heavenly Father; relax and enjoy your time in his presence. Be anxious for nothing (Philippians 4:6).

The word of God instructed us that we are to pray in the Spirit, this means that you are to allow the Holy Spirit to guide you and initiate your prayer (Ephesians 6:18, Jude 1:20 and Romans 8:26). I pray that you will go back to these scriptures in your study time, and read them again for the Holy Spirit to enlighten you, and give you more insight and revelation. Yes, he may lead you to another scripture for an open discussion.

As we draw nigh unto God and come into a relationship, we will learn that God's desire is that we pray for others, our leaders, our nation, etc. As we yield and listen, the Holy Spirit will quicken us to pray and intercede more for others than the things that concerns us. That is why we must allow the Holy Spirit to lead us in our prayer; there is so much that is to be done in the spirit realm for others such as healing, deliverance, salvation, repentance, etc. Before going to the cross, Jesus prayed to God for three things. First, he prayed that God would be glorified in the purpose for which he came and his death on the cross.

Second, Jesus prayed for his disciples' protection and that they would be sanctified in the truth of the word and in him as they went out into the world. Third, Jesus prayed for all believers would we be unified with him and the Father, and for God's love to be in us as it was in him (John 17). As we pray, we must want God to be glorified in the things we are asking and be motivated by God's love to pray for others with the love of God.

We must be obedient to what God speaks to us.

I don't want to assume that everyone has heard that obedience is better than sacrifice (1 Samuel 15:22). God is more concerned if we will do what he asks of us than the sacrifices we bring and offer to him (time, tithes, offerings, work, etc.) Our relationship can't be one-sided where we only want God to bless and do everything for us. We must be willing to listen to God and obey what he speaks to us as well. In my conversations, people have admitted that they don't always wait for God to speak because they are afraid of what he might ask them to do. At least, they are honest to confess, so that is not a time to condemn but to encourage. As you come into a relationship with God, you will learn that he will always have your best interest at heart even when you don't understand. You can't have a relationship with God without a willingness to obey him. It is a trick of the enemy to get you out of relationship with the Father by lying to you about how hard it is or to deceive you by making it look impossible. Obedience is a test of your faith, and the act of surrendering and yielding to God's will. The more you choose to obey, the stronger your relationship will become because you will see the result and the power of what happens when you obey God. Miracles, signs, and wonders are released! The word of God commands our obedience if we say that we love God.

John 14:15 NIV reads, "If you love me, keep my commands." Second John 1:6 KJV tells us that obeying God is how we show the love that we have towards him. It says, "And this is love, that we walk after his commandments. This is the commandment, That, as ye have heard from the beginning, ye should walk in it." Obeying is a choice, like other choices that we face every day. God desire that we choose to obey him. By doing so, we are choosing life in and with him. As long as we live in this world, we will have to choose between life and death, and blessings and curses; there are consequences for each choice. If we are in relationship with God, he will always speak and lead us in everything concerning life and all the blessings of life.

Drawing Nigh Chapter Challenge

There is so much to write concerning the Holy Spirit as our helper, the word of God, prayer, and obedience. I give this challenge as an everyday challenge so that we can come into the fullness of a true, intimate relationship with the Father. We will only walk in a third, half, or three-fourths of our potential relationship without the Holy Spirit, the word, prayer, and obedience. God's desire is that we all come into the fullness of who he is and wants to be in our lives. As we come into relationship, our Father speaks from his written word. Yes, he also speaks a rhema word, but that too results from the written word. The Holy Spirit is a person. Begin to have conversations with him; call him by his name. As we read the word and pray, the Holy Spirit will be at our beck and call for the will and purpose of God to be fulfilled in our lives. What the Holy Spirit hears from the Father, he will speak to us and pray through us.

Chapter 9: Remaining Steadfast in God

As we look all around us, it is so easy to lose focus and forget who we are and the power that has been given to us. When we lose focus, we speak without thinking. We forget that life and death are in the power of our tongue. We ask to be blessed, not understanding that God has blessed us with every spiritual blessing. He is our Jehovah-Jireh, our provider. In the good or the bad times, we must not forget the mighty God we serve. To remain steadfast in him, we must renew our minds daily to what God says about us and the situations we face. We may not have the answers, but we can have his peace and joy as we keep our minds stayed on him. We must decide to let go of this world and understand how to live in the world but not conform to its pattern. We do this by renewing our minds and putting our flesh under subjection to the scriptures and Spirit of God.

In this last chapter, I want to share what God often speaks to me concerning his love for us and how he longs for us to delight ourselves in him. The more we draw nigh unto him, the more of himself he will lavish on us so that we can become more like Jesus. I believe the next few topics need to be fully addressed in separate book, and if allowed by God, I hope to write it one day. From these topics, God wants you to be encouraged. His desire is that you will remain steadfast in him and unified in the spirit so that your relationship with him can continue to be perfected.

God's Love, Grace, & Mercy

God's Love

God's love for us today has not changed. 1 John 3: 1a ABPE says, "And behold how much the love of The Father abounds to us, that he has called us and also has made us children." The world has so many definitions and standards to define love, and the term love is used so loosely. We see that people get married and say that they love each other. However, three months later, they want a divorce. Although God's love is unimaginable and hard to comprehend, we must believe he loves us with our heart, like we believed for our salvation. God's love for us is authentic, genuine, true, pure, and holy.

No matter what we are faced with, or the wrong things we have done, God's love is forever toward us; it is everlasting. God loves us unconditionally. Unconditional love is not governed by emotions or feelings. Unfortunately, most people define love and base their love for others on how they feel. Our emotions and feelings are to express our love for God and others. They should not drive our decision to love.

There are conditions of obedience in his word, but the conditions are to get our character to line up to God's character of love and to love him with all our heart, soul, and might. It is imperative to know that God's love will call for correction and rebuke at times by him and those in authority. His word tells us that he chastises those whom he loves (Hebrews 12:6). But I am a witness! In all my shortcomings and when I failed, God's chastisements and correction toward me brought me peace and joy. There is no condemnation in God's love. There is no shame in God's love. God's correction is 100% motivated by his love.

We should never feel that we must run away from God. I recall meeting with a group of ladies at an "Ashes to Beauty" gathering. God spoke to me one day and said, "Marilyn, for some, it is hard for them to understand and know that I want to turn their ashes into beauty because they don't know that my love for them is unfailing. When they understand my love for them, then they will trust me with their ashes." At that moment, God gave me the assignment to let his children know how much God loves them. Contrary to the lies of the enemy, tradition, and religion that says you have to do this or that, God's love does not come with a measuring stick. If that were the case, no one would or could ever measure up. His love does not put people in bondage or make them feel like they don't measure up.

When God launched my husband and I into ministry, he gave us the name *Unfailing Love Worship Center*. He spoke that love is to always be the foundation, covered with worship. His love for us is unfailing, and if you do not know his love or need to be reminded, declare God's unfailing love over your life.

- But I am like an olive tree flourishing in the house of God; I trust in God's unfailing love for ever and ever. (Psalm 52:8 NIV)

- Show us your unfailing love, O LORD, and grant us your salvation. (Psalm 85:7 NIV)

- May your unfailing love come to me, LORD, your salvation according to your promise. (Psalm 119:41 NIV)

- Within your temple, O God, we meditate on your unfailing love. (Psalm 48:9 NIV)

- Satisfy us in the morning with your unfailing love, that we may sing for joy and be glad all our days. (Psalm 90:14 NIV)

- Let them give thanks to the LORD for his unfailing love and his wonderful deeds for mankind. (Psalm 107:8 NIV)

- May your unfailing love be my comfort, according to your promise to your servant. (Psalm 119:76 NIV)

- In your unfailing love, silence my enemies; destroy all my foes, for I am your servant. (Psalm 143:12 NIV)

- The LORD delights in those who fear him, who put their hope in his unfailing love. (Psalm 147:11 NIV)

In the times that are among us, we need to know how much our Father loves us so that he can direct and order our footsteps. God loves you and desires a relationship where you will know of his love without a shadow of doubt. As you draw nigh, pray his word. "Let the morning bring me word of your unfailing love, for I have put my trust in you. Show me the way I should go, for to you I entrust my life." (Psalm 143:8 NIV)

God's Grace

God did not give us his grace to sin but to have dominion over sin. In Jesus, we have redemption through his blood, the forgiveness of sins, in accordance with the riches of God's grace. (Ephesians 1:7). Our salvation is God's grace; God's grace is a gift. No one can or should ever boast or think that something that they may have done or said merited God's grace. We are living in the dispensation of God's grace, and we are not to take his grace for granted.

God's grace is always sufficient for all that we need and for the times when we are going through trials and tribulations. God's grace strengthens us and is made perfect in weakness (2 Corinthians 12:9-10). His grace is with us even when we don't think we need it or give him glory for it. God does not take his grace away from us. The song writer wrote, "Amazing grace how sweet the sound that save a wretch like me." For every problem and need we face, God's grace is amazing. It is his grace that keep us when we mess up. We can say as Paul said, "But by the grace of God I am what I am." (1 Corinthians 15:10)

It is by the grace of God that we can walk in freedom and liberty. We can't afford to allow tradition and religion to put us into bondage. We are no longer under the law. Romans 6:14 KJV says, "For sin shall not have dominion over you: for ye are not under the law, but under grace." God's grace helps us to become more like Christ.

God's grace has also been given to us so that we can have relationships with him and other people. As God has extended his grace towards us, we must also learn to extend God's grace to others even when they have wronged us. Acts 11:23 KJV says, "Who, when he came, and had seen the grace of God, was glad, and exhorted them all, that with purpose of heart they would cleave unto the Lord." As we draw nigh unto God and grow in our relationship with God, we will see how God's grace has been at work in our lives. We will thank God every day for his grace--his unmerited favor.

God's Mercy

God's mercy is also an act of his grace. Grace and mercy are intertwined with each other. To keep it simple, we will use this definition:

- God's grace gives us what we don't deserve while God's mercy doesn't give us what we do deserve.

God is merciful and gracious, slow to anger, and plenteous in his mercy towards us, but he also wants us to reverence who he is (Psalm 103:8). A lack of reverence for God opens the door for the enemy to make one feel guilty and ashamed. God wants his children to be encouraged through the knowledge of his lovingkindness and compassion that he has for them, whether they be saved or unsaved, or just or unjust (Matthew 5:45). As God has breathed the breath of life into you this day, he wants you to rest in the assurance of knowing that his mercy and goodness is following you. His will and desire is for your heart to be towards him.

God's mercy extends to us the characteristics of his love--joy, peace, longsuffering, gentleness, goodness, and patience. Sometimes, when preaching the gospel of the kingdom, witnessing salvation through Christ, a person will often say they will give their life to Christ, "When I get things right." Even though I explain that no one could make themselves right with God, unbelievers have a hard time believing that God's mercy is extended toward them. The harsh world where everyone wants to get people back for what they have done makes it hard to believe.

God is not like man; he is good to all and has compassion on all he has made in his image (Psalm 145:9). What is even more grieving to God is when we, his children, don't show mercy. Believers are to show God's mercy to everyone just as God extended his mercy toward us when we were in sin. All that God is to us, we are to be to others. God's word is true; with the same measure we judge, we will be judged. We are to forgive seventy times seven and have bowels of mercies and compassion towards everyone. The world will be more accepting of God when we do what is pleasing in God's sight.

Let us thank God that his mercies are new every morning and for his love, grace, and mercy working in our lives daily. During one of my broken moments, I felt as though I was shipwrecked. Feeling like a castaway, I recall the words of the Holy Spirit speaking to me, "God has given unto you his love, grace, and mercy in exchange for your faith, praise, and worship." He enlightened and encouraged me of God's love, grace, and mercy. It was another transformational change in my life. God's love, grace, and mercy is not to hold on to offenses. It does not render evil for evil or an eye for an eye, but love, grace, and mercy are full of forgiveness, longsuffering, and compassion to all you come in contact with or to all who may have wronged you with their actions.

Our Faith, Praise, and Worship

What is faith and why do we need faith? Webster defines faith as "complete trust or confidence in someone or something." The word of God tells us that faith is the substance of things hoped for and the evidence of things not seen (Hebrews 11:1). God has given to each one of us a measure of faith (Romans 12:3). It is not about how much faith we have but what, where, and who is the object of our faith.

For example, we put our measure of faith in things that we buy. We assume the product will do or operate for the purpose for which we paid the price. Okay, to be a little clearer, when you purchase a car, you assume or hope it will work but you don't know it does until you *put* the key in and *turn* the ignition. Each day without thinking about it, it's the same hope and action. Well, that is faith, for some small and for some big (depending on your car), but it is still faith. Some will say, no I can see my car starting. I say no, you do not, you imagine it will. You can't see it starting until you put the key in and turn the ignition and it does. Well, my point is to get you to see Jesus in the same manner, not in comparison but to put your trust and belief in Jesus like you do anything else that you have or love.

We need faith to fulfil the will and purpose of God for our lives. The word of God tells us that without faith it is impossible to please him. Everything we do for God is done through faith. We believe he is who he says he is and that he will do what he says he will do by faith. Faith requires us to believe and trust him. We believe with our heart and trust the rhema and written words God speaks.

You can have one without the other. For example, we all have a measure of faith, but if we don't believe that God can do it and trust him to do it, then it is just faith by word only. Faith requires action on our part, the word tells us that faith without works is dead. The struggles come when we have to put all three into action. Faith, trust, and belief are interchangeable, but most of us struggle with one of the other, making it not possible to please God. God wants us to believe and trust him. He tells us that we are to trust him and lean not to our own understanding, to acknowledge who he is, and he will direct our paths. Whatever God requires of us, we will need God's directions. If we could do it of ourselves, it wouldn't be faith, and it also will not have the full effectiveness, impact, and desired results of God. Hebrews 11 lets us know that Abel, Enoch, Noah, Abraham, Isaac, Jacob, Moses, and even Rahab the prostitute had to walk by faith. They trusted and believed God in the many different processes and actions that God needed to use to fulfill his will and purpose.

Most people give up during the action process or don't follow God's instructions. Then, they say that it wasn't God's will. But whatever God tells you to do or is in his written word, is his will. Let's not forget what happened to Lot's wife. It wasn't God's will for her to die, but it was her not listening and obeying the word of God that caused her death. That is why we must do what God instructs us to do for the results that he desires, not what we desire. When we don't, we pass off what we don't have or achieve because we either blame the devil or say that it wasn't meant to be.

I recall the end of 2018 when God spoke to my husband about purchasing a new house. I had been praying for a retirement home in a location that I had seen about a year and a half earlier. But my husband had said when we moved in 2015, that it would be the last home. I didn't argue or come against my husband, but I kept praying. That December morning, my husband said let's go look for a house. I was hesitant at first, but I wanted to see where it would go. On our ride, he told me what God had spoken to him. After two weekends of looking, he put

$4,000 down in earnest money without our current home even being on the market. I was like oh God, but the Holy Spirit quickly reminded me about what I was believing God for and the pattern in which God moves in our lives. Please pay attention to the patterns in which God operates in your life.

After putting the earnest money down, I knew this would be another faith walk. We signed the contract on December 28, 2018, put our house on the market on January 5, 2019, closed on the new home on February 20, 2019 and closed on our old house on March 8, 2019 before a payment was due (God gets all the glory). But what I want you to know is that the process was not easy. It was tremendous warfare with the enemy, but we had to believe and trust God.

During our process, God revealed that it is in the *process* that most people will give up before he can release the things for which they are believing him. His people give up during actions or when the enemy comes. They stop praying, believing, and trusting him. The process of your faith will require you praying and listening to the voice of the Holy Spirit to guide you through every step. The process will require your obedience to do exactly what he says.

We had to cast down all vain imaginations, the stress of buying a new home, and marriage disagreements that came with the unseen process. We had to stand on the rhema word of God and declare the written word of God and repent at times. I was glad that we didn't have to fight the naysayers because God was moving too quickly before we could really share. Plus, after a couple of Joseph experiences (sharing my dreams with others), I was a little hesitant on speaking anything to anyone. We spent our time in prayer when we weren't disagreeing about our own perceptions of the process (being honest) and waiting to see what God wanted us to do. Be encouraged and when God speaks, have faith and take a stand. Do the work and know that your timing is not God's timing. Be prepare to wait unless God says no. Yes, God will tell you no, but learn to say yes to God when he says no to you. He always knows what is best for us. Little did we both know that the home would also be part of our next assignment

Faith comes by reading and hearing the word of God. We rely upon the Holy Spirit to help us with revelation, enlightenment, and insight on what God is speaking in the word. There is a renewing of the mind that must take place for us to believe, trust, and take God at his word. The more we read the word and believe, the more it will get rooted in our hearts. We live our lives by faith in Christ and what he has done for us (Gal 2:20). And we walk by faith and not by sight (2 Corinthians 5:7). At times, your faith will be tested by God (Abraham) and by Satan, but God has given us his word to stand every test. I don't believe God gives us a test that he knows we will fail. He knew Abraham was going to be willing to sacrifice his son, he knew Job would not go against him, and that Noah would build the ark. But they had to withstand the test to do it. Each test will increase our faith, so whatever God is speaking to you to do, be like Nike and just do it. Whatever you are believing God for, let your faith and hope be in God.

Our Praise

If I asked what is praise, most people would say as Webster defines it, that praise is to express approval or admiration. We believers say, it is an outward expression of thanks to God. But when I read the word of God, I see that praise is also a command given to us. We are instructed to praise the Lord, to give thanks to the Lord, to bless the Lord, to sing unto the Lord, and to lift up the name of the Lord. We do all these things because of who God is in our lives and the things that he has done for us. This doesn't mean that we wait until God does something, but we are to praise him because he did, he can, and he will do it again.

Praise should be a lifestyle. It makes no difference what we are going through, each day we should wake up with a praise on our lips. Our praise should be habitual. Psalm 105 instructs us to praise him because of his faithfulness towards us. The word reminds us of all that God has done for us, and we should rejoice in him because of his marvelous works. If you don't know why or where to start praising him, read the book of Psalms. It is filled with reasons that we should give God praise. We also praise to express our gratefulness towards him. Sometimes, we must look back over our life to see the miracles, signs, and wonders of God. Our salvation alone was a miracle and enough to praise him. When we praise him, we take the focus off ourselves and back on him where it belongs.

God deserves all our praise, and our praise means a lot to God. It says a lot about our relationship with him. Imagine that when you do something for those with whom you are in relationship with, they never say thanks. We all have a part of us that wants to be praised even when we don't say so (if we are honest). If God desires praise, so do we because we are made in his image. What we don't do is get angry and upset if we do not receive the praise. Our motive for what we do is not to be praised and recognized, but we do everything as unto God first. Know that

God will reward you for your acts of love, kindness, and obedience in the work of the ministry or toward another. God is love and he loves and blesses us even when we don't offer up praise.

We teach our children that it is respectful to say thank you, but we get upset when the leader asks us to show God respect by lifting our hands, singing, and blessing the Lord. We should never have to be asked to give God praise when we come into the house of God. We are commanded to "Enter into his gates with thanksgiving, And into his courts with praise. Be thankful to him and bless his name (Psalm 100:4). We don't need a reason to praise God. In the midst of tiredness, trials, tribulations, etc., we still are required to offer a sacrifice of praise. The sacrifice should not be done half-heartedly, but it is a sign to God that even during what I am feeling and going through, I realize that you still deserve the glory and honor. As the songwriter wrote, "Praise is what I do, when I want to be close to you." We recognize that praise is part of our relationship with the Father.

Our Worship

Praise and worship are normally grouped together and can be interchangeable but the two are different. Praise is an outward expression to God for *what he has done*. Worship is also an outward expression to God but for *who he is*. It has nothing to do with what he gives and does for us. Webster defines worship as to honor or show reverence for a divine being or supernatural power. In our worship, we honor God for his majesty, holiness, and love. Jesus points out that we are to worship God in spirit and in truth (John 4:24). Worship is all about our hearts and the actions of our hearts. Our attitudes, and once again, our motives must be right. Jesus said in Matthew 15:8–9 KJV, "People honor me with their lips, but their heart is far from me; in vain do they worship me." We want our worship to be genuine and authentic to God. As we worship, we open our hearts up to the truth of God. Our focus is him. Worship requires yielding and surrendering all of yourself to who he is and his love.

Worship in the form of music, is what we have been created to do. Worship in spiritual songs is one of the highest honors that we can give God. It was lucifer's (Satan's) job. Satan does not like when we worship God and will do everything in his power to stop us from doing what once belong to him. Satan knows how sincere and powerful worship is, so he does his best to keep our mind focused on anything thing that concerns us so we can't tap into the spiritual realm with God. When we worship God in songs, his power manifests, and things begin to happen supernaturally. I will never forget a time when I was in worship. As I worshipped, God allowed me to see a vision of him standing on his throne, and I heard his voice as he said to me softly, "What is it my child, now that you got my attention." I was at awe and didn't ask for anything because just to be in his presence was enough. I say that to encourage you about what happens when you rid yourself of everything to give reverence and honor God.

It is essential to know that there are other forms of worship; it is not just songs of worship, but it is also the acts of our love to God in other areas of our lives such as prayer, studying and applying the word, or just being servants of God to others. The important thing to know is that our worship is always centered on God and motivated by his love, regardless if it is in a song or actions. In the word of God, we can always look to David, who was a worshipper and understood the importance of worshiping and being in a right-standing with God. David wrote, "Teach me your way, LORD, that I may rely on your faithfulness; give me an undivided heart, that I may fear your name." (Psalm 86:11). David also knew what to do when his heart was not right, which was to repent and ask for forgiveness. David asked God to create in him a clean heart and to renew a right spirit within him, not to be cast out of God's presence and for God not to take the Holy Spirit from him (Psalm 51:10). I encourage you to read Psalm 51 in its entirety, but this is a prayer that we should all pray when we have turned our hearts to other things in this world.

Finally, we don't ever discredit someone's worship because we don't know their heart and what God may be doing in their life. God had to correct me on this. He told me not to yell or force the people to worship him because it can lead to false worship. If I am telling you to worship, then I am out of worship because I can't be in two places in worship. I was reminded of my earlier years in church services. There was a time in my life when all I knew to do was praise. Eventually, after realizing and coming into an understanding of the truth of who God is, my praise led me into worship. And my worship led me to draw nigh unto God. Coming into his presence is the beginning of an personal intimate relationship with him.

Drawing Nigh Chapter Challenge

My last challenge to you is for you to remain steadfast in God. Learn more of God's love, grace, and mercy towards you. Be loving and kind to all those you will meet and extend bowels of mercies. Never forget what God has done for you, and be willing to do the same for others. Decide to walk by faith and not by sight; trust and believe in what God says and has for you. Add work to your faith and don't give up on God in your faith process. In all things, give God what he deserves, all your praise and worship with a pure and genuine heart.

Conclusion

In summary, I shared that this book was birthed in prayer. My spirit was grieved by all that was happening in the world. Now, as I am writing this summary, the world is in an uproar because of the coronavirus (COVID-19). Earlier, God so clearly spoke to me that he is in control, and he is yet in control during this coronavirus. He spoke that he is "The Deliverer," and he is in the midst. For all who have an ear to hear, let him hear what the Spirit is saying in this hour. His words to me have not changed, I hear the echo of his voice each day, desiring that his children will draw nigh unto him. The world is waiting for the manifestation of his sons and daughters. God wants to bring his children into sonship—a relationship with him where his kingdom can come, and his will can be done on earth as it is in heaven.

We quote the scripture that our eyes have not seen, and our ears have not heard the good things that God had prepared for them that love him, but we can't stop there. There is a piece in between that says, "neither the things that have entered into the hearts of men." Then, the next verse reads, "but God **has** revealed them to us by his Spirit; that the Spirit searches **all** things, the deep things of God." We don't know anything except the Spirit reveals it unto us. It goes on to say that we have received the Spirit of God and not the spirit of the world that we may know God. We must decide to allow the Holy Spirit to do the work in our lives so that we can come into a mature relationship with God.

In each chapter, I spoke about what God showed and gave me to write. In the first chapter, God addressed and instructed us as believers to humble ourselves, pray, seek his face, and turn from our wicked ways. Then will he hear from heaven, forgive our sins, and heal our land. It is time to stop pointing the finger, judging, condemning, and devouring one another, our leaders, and all mankind. Our desire should be to see people in God's image as God sees them. We all have sinned and fallen short of God's glory. We can't think so highly of ourselves that we don't cry out for all humanity. We must ask God to cleanse our hearts to see people as Jesus saw them on the cross. It is time to pray and cry out for the people of this world, our nation, and Jerusalem.

Let us begin by conducting self-examination, and do it more frequently. No one is exempt. Self-examination is how we grow in our relationship as we allow God to search our hearts. As God speaks to us in prayer, we must be willing to repent and have a heart of repentance. Allow others to repent and let the Holy Spirit work in their lives. God has not given us the authority or power to judge someone's heart. Only God knows the heart of man.

Let us walk in the spirit of forgiveness; it is an amazing and powerful act that brings freedom, love, joy, and peace to our lives. We can't allow the enemy to deceive us into holding grudges and not free ourselves from the strongholds of unforgiveness. Unforgiveness leads to bitterness, anger, and self-righteousness. It opens the door for the enemy to torment and causes all types of havoc in one's life, not to mention sickness.

After repentance, let us move on to asking God for deliverance. We all have issues or something that we need God to deliver us from; the word says if any man says that he has not sinned, he is a liar, and God is *not* in him. Deliverance breaks the chains and strongholds of sinful behaviors. Deliverance belongs to every believer, and it is an ongoing process, so no one can think that they have arrived or are exempt. God is a deliverer, and there is nothing he desires more in this hour than to deliver his people.

Let us seek not to be self-righteous and to think more highly of ourselves than we ought to think. The spirit of tradition and religion has crept its way into the household of faith. Jesus dealt with the Pharisees and Sadducees because they had a form of godliness. They put God's people in bondage with their laws. If we are leaders or in a leadership position, we must know that God has entrusted the care of his children with us. We are to teach, train, and equip the people to become mature in Christ and for the work of the ministry and for the edifying of the body of Christ. Yes, we are to correct and admonish, but all in God's love. Let us get out of the Holy Spirit's position and pray, trust, and believe God for his children.

I want to encourage you that no matter who you are, God cares! Jesus died to redeem us all. The ministry of reconciliation is all about Jesus bringing us back into a relationship with the Father. Everyone was born with a purpose for a purpose, God's purpose! God had predestined and ordained you before you were in your mother's womb. Only he knows the thoughts and plans for you, and they are good. Trust him, it is he who has begun a good work in you, and he will also complete it to the end if you let him.

God wants you to know that his love for you is unfailing. His grace and mercy are always towards you, and the blood of Jesus is your validity in him. Jesus did not leave you comfortless.

When you received Christ, the Holy Spirit dwelt on the inside of you. You are sealed by the Holy Spirit, and you are guaranteed in him. Regardless of how hard things may become in your life, God wants you to know not to run away; his arms are always outstretched towards you. Talk and communicate with the Holy Spirit and ask him to lead and guide you on your journey. You are destined for greatness!

I pray that you will remain steadfast in God. Believe, trust, and have faith in God. Know the beauty of yielding and surrendering unto him. In all things, be grateful and thankful. Always give God what he deserves, all the glory and honor. Lift your praises towards him, and pour your love out on him with your worship.

Purpose in your heart this day to draw nigh unto him, and let go and let God have his way. I promise you, your experience and encounter with Him will be far greater than anything that you can imagine.

Be of good cheer, be good to one another, forbear one another, be merciful, and be quick to forgive everyone. Walk in God's freedom and his love. Pray for all!

My Prayer for You

Our Father, which are in heaven, we honor and glorify you today. We humble ourselves before you and cry out for the healing of our land. We come boldly to the throne of grace, where we can find help and mercy in the time of need. We declare your kingdom to come and your will to be done on earth as it is in heaven. Give us your word on today that will transform our lives. Let us be mindful of the blood of Jesus that was shed for all humanity as we pray and intercede for all. Forgive us; we repent from judging unrighteous from an ungodly place in our hearts and minds. We declare that we will not bring condemnation against your people, but we will walk with a lowly heart, not exalting ourselves more highly than we ought.

We confess that we need you. We acknowledge and give thanks to you as our king, Jesus Christ, our savior and redeemer, and the Holy Spirit, our helper. We pray for your divine nature to take root in our lives as we present our bodies as a living sacrifice, holy and acceptable unto you. Let us not misrepresent you and who you are.

Search our hearts, and prune the areas of our lives where good fruit are not being produced, we want to walk uprightly before you and possess your character. Create in us a clean heart and renew a right spirit within us. We commit our ways to you as we draw nigh unto you. Let our relationship with you be inseparable. Give us your heart and strengthen us to do your will.

Let your love be embedded in our hearts that we will love others, be quick to forgive, and show your mercy and grace.

We pray for our world leaders, church leaders, local and state officials, and our government.

Our faith, trust, hope, and expectations are in you. We push back the forces of evil and come against the power of darkness, wickedness, and every high thing that exalt itself against the knowledge of you, who you are, and whose we are! We shall not be ignorant of Satan's devices, tactics, and schemes.

We cast down vain imaginations, anxiety, fear, doubt, and worry. We stand firm on your word and declare your power, love, and sound mind to be ours.

We declare that we are not conformed to this world and the world systems, but our minds are renewed in Christ. We walk in the power and authority given unto us, and we boldly call those things that be not as though they were. We stand on the truth of your word, and we shall not be move!

We thank you for a life of abundance, and we lack nothing in you. Thank you for the good thoughts and plans you have for us. We declare our prosperity--spiritually, physically, mentally, and financially. Today, our heads are hung high, and our mouths are filled with praise. We worship you in spirit and in truth. We are strong and courageous in you! We are not perplexed. Our hands are clean, and our hearts are pure as we draw nigh unto him. Thank you for an intimate relationship with and in you. In Jesus' name, amen. Amen!

Salvation is for Everyone

If you have never ask Jesus into your life, it is as simple as the word tells us in Romans 10:9-10, that if you confess with your mouth the Lord Jesus and believe in your heart that God has raised Jesus from the dead, you will be saved. For with the heart one believes unto righteousness, and with the mouth confession is made unto salvation.

Pray this prayer, Heavenly Father, I am a sinner and I realized that Jesus is my Savior and was sent to redeemed me and to reconcile me back to you. I believe his blood was shed for me and I am made righteous in Him. Today, I confess that Jesus is Lord and I ask him to become Lord of my life. I believe in my heart that I am made righteous in Christ. I give you permission and I ask for you to transform my life and for the Holy Spirit to help me live a life for Christ, in Jesus name, I pray amen!

Glory to God, the angels in heaven are rejoicing with you. Begin your journey, drawing nigh unto God and communicate with the Holy Spirit for directions for your life and a local church home free from condemnation and religion where you can be train and equipped to mature in Christ and your purpose and all that God has for you.

About the Author

Marilyn was born in 1961 and raised in South Carolina. She is a 1979 graduate, an Air Force retiree, and currently a Federal Service employee with an associate degree in Information and Communication Systems, a bachelor's degree in Human Services, and a master's degree in Human Resources. She accepted Christ into her life at the age of fifteen but rededicated her life on October 18, 1992.

In 1997, she had an encounter with God, where he spoke and called her as his prophet to his people. She takes her calling seriously and has a passion for the people of God to know the voice of the Father, their Savior Jesus Christ, and their present helper, the Holy Spirit.

She has served under various apostles, bishops, and pastors and ministries in the capacities of Sunday School secretary, church treasurer, praise and worship, choir, women's ministry, cleaning ministries, intercessory prayer, bookstore management, and teaching and preaching during services and classes. She received licenses under three ministries but holds to the truth that it is *not* about the title or position rather the function of the call as one is led by God's Spirit, his will, and purpose.

Always remembering what Jesus did for her on the cross, her mission is to love, encourage, exhort, and respect all of God's people, whether believers and non-believers. Her mission is to preach the gospel of the kingdom so all will come into the knowledge and understanding of God's love and purpose for their lives.

In 2007, Marilyn said yes to birthing *Ashes to Beauty Ministries*, and in 2017, *The REAL (Respect~Encourage~Admonish~Love)* which is a forum for everyone dealing with real-life issues to know the truth of God's word from his perspective. Marilyn believes strongly in the teaching of the Holy Ghost and her desire is for people's ears and hearts to be attentive to God in every season of their lives. She gives all the praise, honor and glory to the one and only true God for all that he has done.

She is currently a disciple of Unfailing Love Worship Center, where she serves beside her husband, Apostle Donald J. Haydel, Jr. They have four beautiful children.

For more information Ms. Haydel can be reach at unfailing_love@outlook.com.

www.ingramcontent.com/pod-product-compliance
Lightning Source LLC
LaVergne TN
LVHW051505070426
835507LV00022B/2934